KU-266-433

George Orwell's

Animal Farm

Text by
Joseph E. Scalia
(M.A., Brooklyn College)
Department of English
Hicksville High School
Hicksville, New York

Illustrations by
Karen Pica

Research & Education Association
Dr. M. Fogiel, Director

MAXnotes® for
ANIMAL FARM

Printed in the United States of America

Library of Congress Control Number 00-191848

International Standard Book Number 0-87891-988-0

MAXnotes® is a trademark of
Research & Education Association, Piscataway, New Jersey 08854

What **MAXnotes®** Will Do for You

This book is intended to help you absorb the essential contents and features of Orwell's *Animal Farm* and to help you gain a thorough understanding of the work. Our book has been designed to do this more quickly and effectively than any other study guide.

For best results, this **MAXnotes** book should be used as a companion to the actual work, not instead of it. The interaction between the two will greatly benefit you.

To help you in your studies, this book presents the most up-to-date interpretations of every section of the actual work, followed by questions and fully explained answers that will enable you to analyze the material critically. The questions also will help you to test your understanding of the work and will prepare you for discussions and exams.

Meaningful illustrations are included to further enhance your understanding and enjoyment of the literary work. The illustrations are designed to place you into the mood and spirit of the work's settings.

The **MAXnotes** also include summaries, character lists, explanations of plot, and section-by-section analyses. A biography of the author and discussion of the work's historical context will help you put this literary piece into the proper framework of what is taking place.

The use of this study guide will save you the hours of preparation time that would ordinarily be required to arrive at a complete grasp of this work of literature. You will be well-prepared for classroom discussions, homework, and exams. The guidelines that are included for writing papers and reports on various topics will prepare you for any added work which may be assigned.

The **MAXnotes** will take your grades "to the max."

Dr. Max Fogiel
Program Director

Contents

**Each chapter includes List of Characters,
Summary, Analysis, Study Questions and
Answers, and Suggested Essay Topics.**

MAXnotes® are simply the best – but don't just take our word for it...

"... I have told every bookstore in the area to carry your MAXnotes. They are the only notes I recommend to my students. There is no comparison between MAXnotes and all other notes ..."
  – High School Teacher & Reading Specialist,
  Arlington High School, Arlington, MA

"... I discovered the MAXnotes when a friend loaned me her copy of the *MAXnotes for Romeo and Juliet.* The book really helped me understand the story. Please send me a list of stores in my area that carry the MAXnotes. I would like to use more of them ..."
  – Student, San Marino, CA

"... The two MAXnotes titles that I have used have been very, very useful in helping me understand the subject matter reviewed. Thank you for creating the MAXnotes series ..."
  – Student, Morrisville, PA

A Glance at Some of the Characters

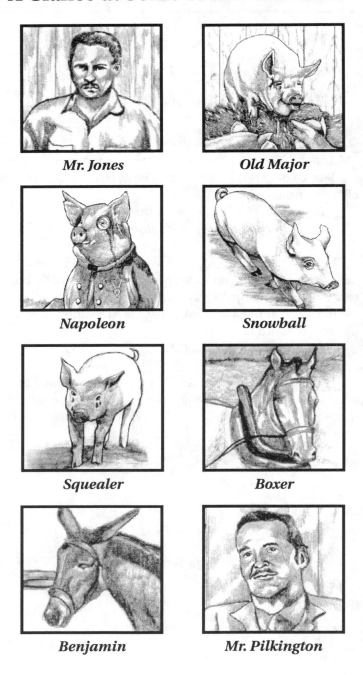

Mr. Jones

Old Major

Napoleon

Snowball

Squealer

Boxer

Benjamin

Mr. Pilkington

SECTION ONE

Introduction

The Life and Work of George Orwell

George Orwell was born Eric Hugh Blair in 1903 in Motihari, Bengal, India. He was the second of three children, and the only boy, born to Richard and Ida Blair. His elder sister, Marjorie, and his younger sister, Avril, completed this middle-class Anglo-Indian family. His dour, discouraging father was an agent in the Opium Department of the British Civil Service. As was the custom with such middle-class children born abroad, he was sent back to England for his education. His mother, a modern, rather left-wing woman and militant suffragette, accompanied him.

Orwell attended the best English schools, including Eton College (1917-1921), a school that epitomized "traditional" British education. Poorer than the other students and feeling insecure about himself, he never quite fit in with the rest of his classmates. Politically, he had difficulty accepting the world of British imperialism that surrounded him. These feelings of being an "outsider," coupled with Orwell's firm belief (which he expressed early in his life to friends and family) that he felt fated to become a "great writer," affected the course of his entire life. Influenced by his mother's "revolutionary" politics and charged by his own political ideas, Orwell ultimately turned to a writing career.

However, when he graduated from Eton College in 1921, Orwell briefly followed the family tradition and entered civil service as a member of the Indian Imperial Police in Burma. He served in this position from 1922 to 1927, gathering material for his two most famous essays, "On Shooting an Elephant" and "A Hanging." During these five years, he witnessed and participated in the British policies of colonialism. A Socialist at heart, Orwell came to the conclusion that British imperialism was futile and destined to come to an end.

Orwell returned to England to devote his time to writing and supported himself in this period of fairly severe poverty with a series of temporary jobs and journalistic writing assignments. An account of these difficult years was recorded in his first book, *Down and Out in Paris and London* (1933). His novel *Burmese Days* (1934) came from his Far East experiences. It was followed by *A Clergyman's Daughter* (1935) and *Keep the Aspidistra Flying* (1936), which expressed his negative attitudes toward British society. An assignment covering the lives of the miners of northern England enabled Orwell to share the experiences and hardships of these working-class people.

Orwell married Eileen O'Shaughnessy in the summer of 1936. At the end of that year, he and his new wife left for Spain where he joined a "Trotskyist" unit of the militia and fought in the Spanish Civil War. What he witnessed there shook his Socialist ideals. He was appalled by the brutal tactics employed by the Communists who were armed by the Soviet Union and turned loose against Stalin's political enemies in Spain. Orwell was wounded in Spain and diagnosed with tuberculosis upon his return to England. An account of his Spanish experiences is the subject of *Homage to Catalonia* (1938), an autobiographical work.

During World War II, Orwell was kept out of active service because of his worsening health. He continued to contribute to the war effort through his writing and his broadcasts to India over the BBC. When his wife died in 1943 during a minor operation, Orwell left London and went to the Hebrides Islands with his adopted son. From November 1943 to January 1944, he worked on *Animal Farm*, which he published in 1945 as the war was coming to an end. His tuberculosis grew worse but his writing continued. He completed *1984*, a political novel which he began in 1948 and saw published in 1949, just six months before his death on January 21, 1950, at the age of 46.

Historical Background

In 1917, as George Orwell was preparing to attend Eton School, two major world events were taking place. Europe was embroiled in a major conflict that later would be called World War I, and Russia was on the brink of a revolution that would have an impact on the planet for the next 75 years. Both events stemmed from a long history of complex political entanglements, secret agreements, and economic considerations. World War I began with the assassination of Archduke Ferdinand in Sarajevo in 1914.

In Russia, the decade leading to the Revolution of 1917 began with a series of Russian defeats in the war with Japan. Military mutinies and workers' strikes culminated in a march on the Tsar's Winter Palace at Petersburg. When workers attempted to present a petition calling for factory reforms and civil and political rights, Tsarist troops opened fire. Ninety-six workers were killed and over 300 were wounded. Another 34 died later. The seeds were sown. In March 1917, the Revolution began, and Russia, economically drained by the cost of the world war and demoralized by defeats in that war, rose against Tsar Nicholas II. In October, the Bolsheviks (Communists) staged a second revolution and seized power.

Among their leaders was Vladimir Ilyich Ulianov (Lenin), a committed revolutionary, who was inspired by the teachings of Karl Marx (1818-1883). Marx, a German economist and the author of *Das Kapital* and co-author of *The Communist Manifesto*, called for a struggle of the proletariat (workers) against the aristocracy. The ensuing years of political struggle and civil war brought about the rise to power of Leon Trotsky and Josef Stalin, as well as the arrest and murder of the Tsar and his entire family. The next two decades brought the death of Lenin in January 1924. A power struggle between Trotsky and Stalin ensued. It ended with Trotsky's deportation from the Soviet Union in 1929, and his assassination in Mexico City in 1940. Under the new Communist regime, the people suffered through famine and civil war. Stalin's taking despotic control of the country after a series of public trials in the 1930s to "purge" the government of his political enemies furthered that suffering.

Reaction to the Novel

When *Animal Farm* was completed in February 1944, it was offered to Victor Gollancz of the Left Book Club, whose book choices were distributed to more than 40,000 readers. The offer was refused. However, it was a decision Gollancz later regretted as a professional publishing mistake, for the work became one of the few undoubted masterpieces of our time. It is viable as a work of fiction that one can read and appreciate with no historical background, and as a simple, classic story of struggle against tyranny and the corruption of power. It also belongs to the *genre* of allegory; Orwell himself subtitles *Animal Farm* "A Fairy Story." In developing his characters—barn animals and people on the Manor Farm in England—and the events of the story—the oppression of the animals, the ultimate subversion of their dream for change, and the victory of tyranny over idealism—Orwell renders a faithful view of Russian history and world politics from 1917 to 1943.

His story symbolically depicts Russia under the rule of the Tsars; the Communist Revolution of 1917; the War of Intervention where British, American, and French forces attempted to intervene in the events and affect the outcome of the Russian Civil War; the New Economic Plan to modernize the Soviet Union and lead it into the twentieth century; Stalin's first Five Year Plan; the power struggle within the Communist party that brought about the expulsion of Trotsky and the dictatorship of Stalin; the "Great Purge" of 1937-38; the Hitler-Stalin Pact of 1939; the German invasion of the Soviet Union in 1941; World War II; and the subsequent uneasy friendship between Stalin and the allied leaders during that war.

Coincidentally, *Animal Farm* came into existence the same year that the atomic bomb hit Hiroshima and Nagasaki. According to a review by C. M. Woodhouse published in *The Times Literary Supplement* in London on August 6, 1954, it has had nearly as much impact.

> ... Orwell's still, small voice has also made itself continuously heard in its own quiet, persistent, almost nagging way.... Already in a score of countries and dozen languages *Animal Farm* has made its peculiar mark in translation and in strip-car-

toon...; and the political flavor of its message... has not been lost in the transcription. Already Orwell has launched the 'long haul' of wresting back some of those cardinal, once meaningful, words like 'equality,' 'peace,' 'democracy,' which have been fraudulently converted into shibboleths of political warfare; and already it is impossible for anyone who has read *Animal Farm* (as well as for many who have not) to listen to the demagogues' claptrap about equality without also hearing the still, small voice that adds... but some are more equal than others.

The book was promptly condemned by Josef Stalin and banned in the Soviet Union.

Master List of Characters

Mr. Jones—*the owner of the Manor Farm in England, an alcoholic who treated his animals poorly; Tsar Nicholas II.*

Old Major—*the prize Middle White Boar who identifies man as the cause of all the animals' problems, formulates the ideals of Animalism, and calls for revolution against man; Karl Marx.*

Napoleon—*fierce-looking Berkshire boar who becomes the tyrannical leader of Animal Farm; Josef Stalin.*

Snowball—*vivacious pig leader of Animal Farm and military tactician who is run off the farm by Napoleon; Leon Trotsky.*

Squealer—*a fat porker and a convincing speaker who becomes Napoleon's "mouthpiece." He assuages the fears and doubts of the other animals and it is said that he can turn "black into white"; Soviet propaganda.*

Boxer—*loyal, hard-working horse who believes in the Revolution and everything Napoleon says; the loyal proletariat.*

Benjamin—*cynical donkey and friend of Boxer who thinks life will continue to go badly, even after the revolution; the "silent majority" who didn't protest, but did what was necessary to survive under the Tsar or under Stalin.*

Clover—*stout mare and friend of Boxer.*

Mollie—*Mr. Jones's cart horse who is vain and fond of ribbons, special treatment and lump sugar; the aristocracy under the Tsar.*

Bluebell—*a dog whose pups are taken and trained by Napoleon.*

Jessie—*another dog whose pups are taken by Napoleon.*

Pincher—*a third dog.*

Muriel—*the white goat who learns how to read.*

Moses—*the raven and spy for Mr. Jones who tells and animals about Sugar Candy Mountain, a place where they won't have to work and where they will have all the food they want; the Church in Russia.*

Sheep—*followers of Napoleon who are taught by Squealer to call out slogans at critical moments.*

Minimus—*a pig who writes poems about Napoleon.*

Mr. Pilkington—*the owner of Foxwood farm, who tries to help Jones recover his farm after the Rebellion; Churchill and Great Britain.*

Mr. Frederick—*the owner of Pinchfield farm who later blows up the windmill; Hitler and Germany.*

Mr. Whymper—*the agent who sees an opportunity to make money by helping Napoleon carry on trade with the outside world; Capitalists.*

Summary of the Novel

The animals of Manor Farm have always been miserable under Mr. Jones and his men. They have come to accept their difficult lives as part of the natural order of things. It is Old Major, a prize-winning boar, who shares his dreams with the other animals. He tells them that the cause of all their suffering is man. With man gone, the animals would enjoy the abundance the land provides and build a new society based on equality. He says that Jones has no concern for the animals—that he uses them until they are no longer productive. He butchers the pigs and drowns the dogs when they get old. Old Major predicts that Jones will even sell Boxer, the horse, and the hardest and most faithful worker on the farm, to the slaughterhouse once he is no longer able to work. He encourages the animals to work for this revolution. He warns them never to become like man and to always treat each other as equals.

Three nights later, Old Major dies, and the task of preparing the animals for the revolution falls to the pigs, who are smarter than the others and who later teach themselves to read. Three young pigs, the intellectual Snowball, the domineering Napoleon and the eloquent Squealer, organize Old Major's dream of the future into a political philosophy called Animalism.

When the drunken Mr. Jones fails to feed the animals one night, the animals drive him and his men off the farm. They change the name to "Animal Farm," and the pigs, who seem to have assumed leadership, write the principles of Animalism, reduced to Seven Commandments, on the barn wall. These are to be the unalterable rules by which the animals will live ever after:

1. Whatever goes upon two legs is an enemy.
2. Whatever goes upon four legs, or has wings, is a friend.
3. No animal shall wear clothes.
4. No animal shall sleep in a bed.
5. No animal shall drink alcohol.
6. No animal shall kill any other animal.
7. All animals are equal.

At first the revolution seems to be a success. All of the animals, directed and supervised by the pigs, work hard to bring in the harvest. But there are indications from the beginning that the pigs treat themselves specially. They remain the supervisors, doing no physical labor, and they take extra food (mild and windfall apples) for themselves instead of sharing with the others. Meanwhile Jones, with the aid of his neighbors, tries to retake the farm. They are driven off at the "Battle of the Cowshed" by the military tactics of Snowball and the strength of Boxer. Both are decorated as heroes for their roles in the victory.

A power struggle for control of Animal Farm develops between Snowball and Napoleon, and it culminates with the building of a windmill. When the animals seem about to vote in favor of the project, Napoleon, who opposes the plan, unleashes nine dogs he has been training secretly to follow his orders without question. Snowball is chased off the farm, barely escaping the jaws of the dogs. In a turnabout, Napoleon orders that work on the windmill begin. The work is difficult, and the animals suffer in the process. When a storm blows the windmill down, Napoleon blames the exiled Snowball and condemns him as an enemy. Napoleon exploits the animals' fear that Jones will return and their fear of his fierce dogs to consolidate his power. He uses Squealer to lie to the animals and convince them that things aren't what they seem. As work on the second windmill begins, Napoleon and the pigs become more and more corrupt. They change the commandments, move into Jones's house, and drink whisky. Napoleon even kills other animals who dare to stand up to his authority.

The second windmill is blown up in an attack by Frederick, after he steals wood from Animal Farm, by paying for it with counterfeit money. But Napoleon pronounces this defeat to be a great victory, and work begins on a third attempt to build a windmill. None of the promises of leisure time and comfort come true—no heat or electricity in the barn, no machines to do their hard work. In fact, life grows harder for all of the animals, except the pigs, and food is scarcer. When Boxer, the hardest worker on the farm, is hurt, Napoleon sells him to the horse slaughterer. Squealer convinces the others that Boxer died in the hospital after getting the best treatment. Old Major's prediction about Boxer has come true, but it is Napoleon who is the villain.

In the end, the pigs completely subvert the ideals of Animalism. They are the new masters. They walk on two legs. They violate and change each of the Seven Commandments. Ultimately, these commandments are erased and replaced with only one: "All animals are equal, but some animals are more equal than others." In the final scene, Mr. Pilkington comes for a tour and Napoleon announces some changes. The name is changed back to "Manor Farm," and a new level of understanding is reached between pig and man. The book ends when someone cheats in a card game. The animals, watching from outside, cannot tell the difference between the pigs and the men.

Estimated Reading Time

Animal Farm is a relatively short book of about 130 pages in 10 chapters. Each chapter is approximately 12 pages long. By breaking your reading time into five half-hour segments, two chapters at a sitting, you can read the book in three hours.

Chapter I

New Characters:

Mr. Jones: *the owner and operator of the Manor Farm*

Old Major: *prize Middle White boar and founder of Animalism*

Bluebell, Jessie, and Pincher: *farm dogs*

Boxer: *a horse who is the hardest worker on the farm*

Clover: *a stout motherly mare*

Muriel: *a white goat*

Benjamin: *an ill-tempered, taciturn donkey who is the oldest animal on the farm*

Mollie: *foolish white mare who pulled Jones's cart*

Moses: *the tame raven, Mr. Jones's special pet and spy*

Summary

After Mr. Jones locks the henhouse for the night and goes to bed, the animals of the Manor farm meet in the barn to hear what Old Major, the prize Middle White boar, has to say. Major identifies man as the cause of all the problems for the animals. It is man alone who consumes without producing. Get rid of man, he says, and animals will be rich and free. Jones abuses his animals. Old Major predicts that even Boxer will be sold to the knacker to be boiled down for glue and dog food "the very day that those great muscles of yours lose their power." He formulates his ideas into what will become the principles of Animalism. "All men are en-

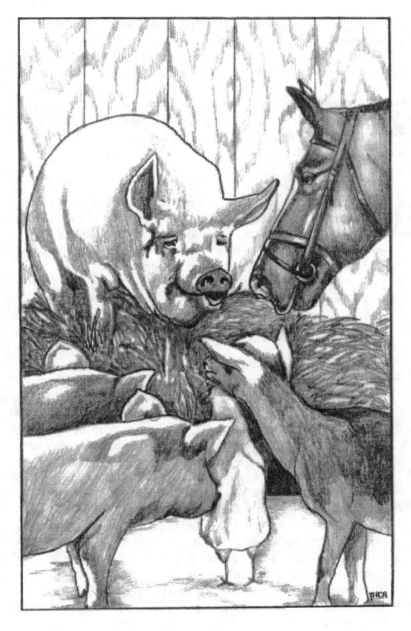

emies. All animals are comrades." He warns them never to become like man in their struggle for freedom and equality, never live in a house, never sleep in a bed, never wear clothes, never drink, smoke or engage in trade. Above all, all animals are equal, and no animal must tyrannize over his own kind. Old Major's dream is of a world without man. He teaches them the revolutionary song *Beasts of England.* The meeting breaks up when Jones, awakened by the up-roar, fires his shotgun and the animals hurriedly return to their sleeping places.

Analysis

On the most basic level, *Animal Farm* is the story of talking farm animals and their struggle against a cruel master. In the open-ing chapter Old Major reveals his dream of utopian society, a place where the animals will be able to live out their lives to their natural ends. It is a society without tyranny, where all animals are "com-rades," equal in every respect. His prediction that Jones will have Boxer slaughtered, the very day he is no longer useful, is very sig-nificant. It will come true, with a most important difference, later in the book. In addressing the animals, Old Major reveals his ideas for a better world after a revolution to overthrow man. Old Major warns them not to become like man once man is gone, nor to be corrupted by power. These principles the pigs later formulate into a theory called Animalism.

But *Animal Farm* is not just a simplistic story. Orwell himself calls it "A Fairy Story." It is a fable, an allegory, a historical satire, where characters and events are symbols that have another level of meaning. Orwell chose the fable form, a technique used by Aesop and others, to teach a concept, a moral, or a lesson in simple terms that an audience could easily understand. A fable uses animal char-acters to represent people. The animals behave like people in ev-ery respect. They talk and have human strengths and weaknesses because, in reality, they are people. Since the purpose of the fable is to instruct, Orwell used the fable form in *Animal Farm* to teach a political lesson to his audience, to portray the events in Russian history from 1917 to 1943. Virtually everything, every character and event in the story, has historical significance. In this allegory, Manor Farm is Russia. Mr. Jones, the owner of the farm, represents Tsar

Nicholas II, the Russian king in 1917. Old Major is Karl Marx, the German political philosopher who formulated the theories that were to become the basis of modern-day communism. Animalism is communism or bolshevism.

One of the themes running through the book is the idea of the "dream betrayed." Chapter I gives the animals hope for a better life without man. Old Major paints a picture of peace and harmony. Ironically, even before the revolution takes place on the farm, before Old Major gives his speech to the ensemble, there are indications that his call for equality, his view of Utopia will never become a reality. Already there are signs that the pigs are different. They are smarter and more clever than the others. Among the first to arrive, the pigs assume a place in the front of the meeting. While Clover is protecting the lost ducklings, other animals are fighting about the status of the wild creatures, the rats and rabbits, in the new society. These are the first examples of foreshadowing, a hint about what is to come in the novel. Perhaps it is Orwell's way of suggesting that true equality never will exist.

Study Questions

1. What is the setting for the story?

2. What four characteristics are noted about Boxer the horse?

3. What comment does Benjamin the donkey make that shows his cynicism and bad temper?

4. How does Clover help the other animals at the meeting?

5. What does Old Major say is the reason the animals have such miserable lives?

6. What is Major's prediction about Boxer.

7. What decision is made concerning the status of wild creatures such as rats and rabbits?

8. What is the name of the song Old Major teaches the animals?

9. What are the main ideas expressed in Major's speech?

10. What indications does Orwell give in this chapter that indicate the pigs may be superior to the other animals?

Answers

1. The setting is the Manor Farm in England.

2. Boxer is an enormous horse. He is respected for his steadiness of character, as well as his tremendous powers and his ability to work. But he is not of first-rate intelligence.

3. He says that God gave him a tail to keep off the flies, but he would rather have no tail and no flies.

4. Clover protects the lost ducklings by making a wall around them with her legs to keep them from getting trampled by the others.

5. Old Major identifies man as the cause of all the animals' problems. Man takes without producing, and he controls the miserable lives of the animals.

6. Old Major predicts that Jones will sell Boxer to the horse slaughterer the day his muscles lose their power and he is no longer useful to Jones.

7. A vote is taken and it is decided that the wild creatures such as rats and rabbits are "comrades."

8. The song is called *Beasts of England*, and it will later become the song of the Rebellion.

9. The main ideas of his speech include the concepts that man is the enemy and all animals are friends. He warns the animals not to become like man, live in houses, wear clothes, drink alcohol, smoke tobacco, touch money, or engage in trade. He says that all animals are brothers, all are equal, and one animal must never tyrannize over his own kind.

10. The pigs sit down in the front row before Major's platform. They are described as being more clever than the other animals, and are able to memorize all the words of *Beasts of England*.

Suggest Essay Topics

1. Major cautions the animals not to resemble man. Yet by creating animals who speak and reason, Orwell has endowed

them with two characteristics which are thought to separate people from humans. Why do you think he does this?
Does the ability to speak or to reason lead to any of the vices
that Major attributes to humans?

2. Research the life and work of Karl Marx. What were the fun-
damentals of his *Communist Manifesto* and how do they
compare to the ideas expressed by Old Major in *Animal
Farm*.

SECTION TWO

Chapter II

New Characters:

Napoleon: *one of the pig leaders, a fierce-looking Berkshire boar, not much of a talker, but with a reputation of getting his own way*

Snowball: *another pig leader, vivacious and inventive*

Squealer: *a fat pig who is a persuasive talker*

Summary

Three nights after giving his speech, Old Major dies in his sleep. The work of organizing the animals falls to the pigs, the cleverest of the animals. Preeminent among the pigs are Napoleon, Snowball and Squealer, who have formed Old Major's teachings into a system of thought called Animalism. Among the difficulties they face is a sense of loyalty some of the animals feel for Mr. Jones. Other animals are apathetic and indifferent.

Mollie, the cart horse, is concerned that she won't have ribbons and sugar after the Rebellion. Their most difficult problem is in counteracting the lies of Moses, the raven. He tells about Sugarcandy Mountain, a place full of clover, lump sugar, and linseed cakes, where the animals will go after they die. The pigs have to convince the others that such a place doesn't exist. The horses, Boxer and Clover, are the most faithful disciples of Animalism. They absorb and believe everything they are told and pass it on to the other animals in simple arguments.

The Rebellion occurs sooner than expected. When Jones, who

has turned to drink, neglects his farm, and forgets to feed the animals, they break into the barn and help themselves. Jones and his men, armed with whips, are unable to regain control and are driven off the farm. When the animals realize what they have done, they gallop around the farm gathering and burning all the implements and symbols of man's control over the animals—whips, nose rings, chains, knives and ribbons. They tour the farmhouse, locking the door and turning it into a museum. They change the name from "Manor Farm" to "Animal Farm." With the others looking on, Snowball paints the Seven Commandments, the unalterable laws that are to govern the animals, on the barn wall. They are:

1. Whatever goes upon two legs is an enemy.
2. Whatever goes upon four legs, or has wings, is a friend.
3. No animal shall wear clothes.
4. No animal shall sleep in a bed.
5. No animal shall drink alcohol.
6. No animal shall kill any other animal.
7. All animals are equal.

Before going into the hayfield to bring in the harvest, the pigs milk the cows and collect five buckets. The animals, hoping for a share of the milk, are sent by Napoleon to bring in the harvest. When they return, the milk is gone.

Analysis

The hungry animals, who have been organized and instructed by the pigs, the leaders of the Rebellion, automatically join together to kick Jones and his men off the farm. After they secure the farm, the animals destroy all of the symbols of Jones's control over them, including the ribbons that Mollie is so fond of wearing on market days. They change the name of their farm and enumerate the laws by which they will govern themselves. The last of these is "All animals are equal." But there are indications that this isn't so. The pigs, specifically Napoleon and Snowball, have become the leaders because they are smarter.

When the milk disappears at the end of the chapter, it is only the first in a series of events to establish the inequality that is de-

veloping between the pigs and other animals. Later in the book, the mystery of the disappearing milk will be explained by Squealer. Napoleon's brewing competition with Snowball is hinted at in the chapter. Napoleon orders Snowball to lead the animals to the hayfield to gather in the harvest while he remains behind with the milk. In the evening when they return, the milk is gone and nothing is said.

Orwell uses the voice of a detached observer to narrate his story. He doesn't judge, but presents events without commentary and allows his readers to come to their own conclusions. But Orwell's simple "fairy story" style is a mask for his cutting political satire. Napoleon, whose very name suggests power and authority, is a composite of Lenin and Stalin, leaders of the Soviet Union after the Communist Revolution. Lenin, who died in 1924, was followed by the ruthless Josef Stalin, whose power lasted until his death in 1953. Snowball is Leon Trotsky, a military tactician and Russian leader. After Lenin's death, a power struggle developed between Trotsky and Stalin and ended when Trotsky was expelled from the Communist party, was exiled and eventually assassinated by an agent of the Soviet Secret Police in Mexico City. Although Squealer is not a specific person, he represents the propaganda (managed information and the controlled media) used by the Soviet government to inform the people, manipulate news, and change history to suit Stalin's needs.

Clover and Boxer represent those peasants who believed strongly in the ideals of the Revolution. And although they may have been misled by corrupt leaders, they worked hard for the cause. Moses stands for the Russian Orthodox Church which enjoyed a position of power under the protection of the tsars. Sugarcandy Mountain is Moses' version of heaven, the reward for those who obey laws. After the Revolution, the Russian Church was disbanded by the Communists. Many priests were exiled, jailed, or executed. Later, when conditions in the Soviet Union deteriorated, the Church was allowed to reopen under strict government scrutiny. Many of the priests were agents who acted as government spies.

Study Questions

1. What happens to Old Major?

2. Who are Napoleon, Snowball, and Squealer?

3. What qualities do they each possess?

4. What are some of the problems the pigs have to face in organizing the other farm animals?

5. Who is Moses and what role does he play on the farm?

6. What is Sugarcandy Mountain?

7. What is the immediate cause of the Rebellion?

8. What are the immediate results of the Rebellion?

9. What are the Seven Commandments?

10. What early indication does Orwell give to show that not all of the animals are treated equally?

Answers

1. Old Major dies peacefully in his sleep.

2. Napoleon, Snowball, and Squealer are the three pig leaders who assume the roles of teaching Old Major's ideas to the other animals.

3. Napoleon is large and fierce, not much of a talker, but accustomed to getting his way. Snowball is vivacious, quick in speech and inventive, but lacking Napoleon's "depth of character." Squealer is a brilliant talker, who is persuasive and capable of turning black into white.

4. Some of the animals feel a duty of loyalty to Jones as the master who feeds them. Some of the animals are indifferent about some vague future rebellion. Some animals are concerned for their own personal comforts.

5. Moses is the tame raven, a special pet of Jones, who feeds him bread soaked in beer. Moses is a spy for Jones.

6. Moses tells the animals about Sugarcandy Mountain, a country full of clover, sugar, and linseed cakes. He says it is where the animals will go when they die.

7. Jones has neglected the animals, drinking rather than working the farm. His farm hands go hunting one day, and the animals are left without food.

8. Jones and his men are driven off the farm. The animals bury the bodies of their slaughtered comrades and burn the things Jones used to control the animals. They change the name from "Manor Farm" to "Animal Farm" and write the Seven Commandments on the barn wall.

9.   1. Whatever goes upon two legs is an enemy.
      2. Whatever goes upon four legs, or has wings, is a friend.
      3. No animal shall wear clothes.
      4. No animal shall sleep in a bed.
      5. No animal shall drink alcohol.
      6. No animal shall kill any other animal.
      7. All animals are equal.

10. Instead of being shared equally among all of the animals, the milk disappears. It is implied that Napoleon takes it for himself.

Suggested Essay Topics

1. Research the life of Vladimir Ilyich Lenin. What role did he play in the Russian Revolution of 1917 and what was his role in the government after the Revolution?

2. Research the life of Josef Stalin. What part did he play during the Revolution? What was his role in the Soviet government through World War II?

3. Research the life of Leon Trotsky. What was his role during the Revolution and after in the Soviet Union? What was his relationship to Lenin and Stalin?

Chapter III

New Characters:

Sheep: *unintelligent animals who follow the leader*

Summary

The days after the Rebellion are good for the animals. All of the animals work hard to bring in the harvest, except the pigs, who direct and supervise. The harvest is a bigger success then Jones and his men had ever had. The animals are happy, and the food they eat is their own. Boxer is the hardest worker. His answer to any problem is, "I will work harder!", which he adopts as his personal motto. The others work according to their abilities, with a few exceptions. Mollie gets up late and leaves early, and the cat has a way of disappearing. Benjamin is the only animal who seems unchanged, slow and obstinate, never shirking and never volunteering. He is fond of saying, "Donkeys live a long time. None of you have ever seen a dead donkey." There is no work on Sunday, and at the weekly meetings, the animals salute their new flag and debate the resolutions put forth by the pigs Napoleon and Snowball, who are never in agreement on any of the issues. The pigs, who have taught themselves to read, set aside the harness room as a headquarters to study blacksmithing, carpentry, and other skills necessary to operate the farm. Snowball organizes committees to increase production and teach the others to read. Napoleon concerns himself with the education of the young, taking nine puppies from their mothers, Jessie and Bluebell, and hiding them away in the loft. The animals learn to read according to their limited

abilities. The sheep learn a single maxim which embodies the essential principles of Animalism: "Four legs good, two legs bad." Once they learn it, they say it for hours.

The animals solve the mystery of the milk. It is mixed every day into the pigs' mash. The milk and the windfall apples are reserved exclusively for the pigs. Squealer explains the necessity for this. Because the pigs are brain workers, the whole management and organization of the farm depends on them. Squealer says that it has been scientifically proven that milk and apples are essential to the well-being of a pig. Even though some pigs don't even like milk and apples, Squealer says, they eat them for the safety and the benefit of the other animals. He ends his argument with the threat that if the pigs fail in their duties, Jones will return. "Surely, comrades, surely there is no one among you who wants to see Jones come back?" The milk and the apples are the only issue that Napoleon and Snowball agree upon. So it is settled without further protest that the apples and milk be put aside for the pigs.

Analysis

The Communists exhorted the peasants to revolt in 1917 with the promise, "Workers of the world unite. You have nothing to lose but your chains." The rebellion of the animals was also based on the ideal that their miserable lives could and would be better. Immediately after the expulsion of Jones, this appears to be the case. But the first test is the harvest. Since the animals are now working for themselves, they bring in the biggest harvest ever in two days' less time than usually took Jones and his men. There is no waste, as every animal, except the pigs, works, "And not an animal on the farm had stolen so much as a mouthful."

It appears that Old Major's dream will come true. Their commitment to the cause is visible in all of the barn animals, but it is most evident in Boxer. Already the hardest worker of the farm, he is always ready to work harder. But there are some indications of problems. The pigs, the new leaders on the farm, do no labor. They are the administrators, the new upper class in a theoretically classless society. How fitting and how sardonic for Orwell to select pigs to represent the leaders of the Communist party, the "new Russian aristocracy."

The struggle for power among Lenin, Stalin, and Trotsky is symbolized by the conflict among the animals. And there are other problems. Mollie, Jones's pampered cart horse, does little work. This is also true of the cat, an opportunist who does no work and only shows up for meals. Historically, Mollie represents the "old Russian aristocracy" who owned the land, controlled the wealth, and enjoyed the protection of the Tsar. After the Revolution of 1917, many of these aristocrats were arrested, re-educated, or executed. Those who could, fled the country to Europe and the United States. It is Benjamin, the symbol of the Russians who suffered under the Tsar and Communism, that grudgingly does whatever is necessary. Benjamin doesn't believe that change is possible, and he has no faith in the new order. His only interest is his own survival.

The coming rift between Napoleon and Snowball, suggestive of the conflict between Stalin and Trotsky, begins to surface in this chapter. Their conflict stems from a difference in ideology as the two try to build their personal power bases on the farm. Snowball works to organize the animal committees and to teach them how to read. Napoleon calls for the education of the youth, and takes the nine puppies to be raised for his own purposes. These dogs, in reality the Russian Secret Police, will appear later and play an important part in Napoleon's grab for total control of the farm. The pigs are called "brain workers" by the eloquent Squealer, whose role as the apologist for the pigs and Napoleon's mouthpiece, is established here.

The chapter also shows the importance of propaganda and the use of managed, slanted information to attain a political end. Squealer is able to head off any complaints by making them believe that the unselfish pigs are acting in the best interest of the farm by eating the apples and drinking the milk. He also relies on the animals' fear by linking the pigs' actions to the return of Jones. But how could all the others be so naive? Because they are misinformed, because they are ignorant, because they are afraid, but most important, because they are trusting.

The years following the Revolution of 1917 were filled with turmoil, civil war, the execution of Tsar Nicholas II and his entire family, and a power struggle between Trotskyites, Stalinists, Socialists, and Bolsheviks. Through it all the peasants struggled to survive.

Study Questions

1. What is the result of the harvest after the Rebellion and why?

2. What part do the pigs play in the harvest?

3. What is Boxer's personal motto?

4. What is the attitude of Mollie and the cat toward work on the farm?

5. What is Benjamin's attitude after the rebellion?

6. What is Benjamin fond of saying and what does it mean?

7. What committees does Snowball organize on the farm?

8. What is the maxim that Snowball teaches the sheep?

9. How does Napoleon deal with "the education of the young"?

10. What happened to the milk taken from the cows, and how does Squealer explain this to the other animals?

Answers

1. Immediately after the Rebellion, the harvest is better than it ever was under Jones because all of the animals (with few exceptions) work hard for their own food.

2. The pigs are the supervisors, directing the other animals in their work.

3. Boxer's personal motto is, "I will work harder."

4. Mollie gets to work late and makes excuses to leave early, and the cat disappears whenever there is work to be done. She reappears at meal time with such good excuses and purrs so affectionately that the others believe her good intentions.

5. Benjamin remains unchanged, cynical, and obstinate. He does no more and no less than he has to do.

6. Benjamin says, "Donkeys live a long time. None of you has ever seen a dead donkey." He is the oldest animal on the farm and he plans to do whatever is necessary to stay alive.

7. Snowball forms the "Egg Production Committee" for the

hens, the "Clean Tails League" for the cows, the "Wild Comrades' Re-education Committee" to tame the rats and rabbits, and the "Whiter Wool Movement" for the sheep, and institutes classes in reading and writing.

8. Their maxim is "Four legs good, two legs bad," which they bleat for hours at a time.

9. He takes the nine puppies and makes himself responsible for their education. After a while, the other animals forget all about the puppies.

10. The pigs get the milk as well as the apples. Squealer explains that it is necessary for the pigs to keep the farm going. If they don't get the milk and apples, Jones will come back.

Suggested Essay Topics

1. Compare the different attitudes of Napoleon and Snowball in Chapter III of the novel. What do they reveal about each of the characters? How do the other animals respond to each of them?

2. Animal Farm is based on actual events which occurred in Russia, each animal or group of animals represents either historical figures or groups of people. By Chapter III, differences in personality and intelligence are established among the animals. How does this relate to Orwell's portrayal of people? Do you think he is suggesting that certain kinds of people are more intelligent or capable than others?

Chapter IV

New Characters:

Mr. Pilkington: *neighbor of Animal Farm and owner of Foxwood Farm*

Mr. Frederick: *neighbor of Animal Farm and owner of Pinchfield Farm*

Summary

As the news of the Rebellion on Animal Farm spreads across the countryside, the animals on neighboring farms become unmanageable. The stories unnerve the neighboring farmers, Mr. Pilkington, the owner of Foxwood Farm, and Mr. Frederick of Pinchfield Farm. Although Pilkington and Frederick are on permanently bad terms with each other, they are sufficiently frightened by the recent events to overcome their differences long enough to join forces with Mr. Jones in an attempt to help him retake the Manor Farm (as they insist on calling it).

The pigeons bring word of the humans' imminent attack, long expected by the animals. Snowball, who has studied an old book of Julius Caesar's military campaigns, is in charge of the defenses of Animal Farm and puts his strategy into action. The humans, tricked into believing that the animals are in retreat, rush into the battle. Quickly they are surrounded and defeated by the well-disciplined and well-organized animal forces. The two heroes are Snowball, who is wounded by pellets fired from Jones's gun, and Boxer. For their roles in the Battle of the Cowshed, as it is called,

they are each awarded a military decoration of "Animal Hero, First Class." A sheep, who is killed in the battle, is posthumously awarded an "Animal Hero, Second Class" medal.

Analysis

Leon Trotsky was the military genius who built the Soviet Army and planned the military campaigns that gave victory to the Communists in the civil war that followed the Revolution. He is personified in Snowball, the first-class hero of the Battle of the Cowshed. It is Snowball who has foreseen the possibility of humans attempting to retake the farm and has planned for it by reading Julius Caesar's battle strategies. The importance of the battle is recognized by Orwell, who devotes more time to it than he does the Rebellion. With the Battle of the Cowshed, Orwell has combined several events from the closing years of World War I and years immediately after the Russian Revolution.

After the abdication of Tsar Nicholas II in 1917, the new Russian government pursued peace with Germany. But when Trotsky rejected the peace terms, Germany launched an attack and occupied territory deep inside Russia until December 1918. At about the same time, the Russian Civil War (1918-1920) broke out between the Communist "Reds" and anti-Communist "Whites." The allied powers, including the United States, Great Britain and France (who were still at war with Germany), and Japan invaded Russia and occupied Russian territory. After the defeat of Germany, the Allied forces remained in Russia and aided the Whites against the Reds. Coming under attack by combined Russian troops, the foreign forces withdrew in 1919, and victory in the Civil War went to the Communists. From it all, Trotsky emerged as a powerful leader, the main architect of the new Red Army. It put him into direct conflict with Stalin and set the stage for their future confrontation which would result in Trotsky's expulsion from the Party and his eventual exile and execution.

In this chapter Orwell introduces the character of Pilkington, the neighboring farmer and the owner of Foxwood Farm, to represent Great Britain and British Minister of War (and future Prime Minister), Winston Churchill. It was Churchill who early recognized the threat posed by communism and advocated the Allied invasion of Russia. Frederick represents Germany, and later Adolf Hitler who came to power in the 1930s and remained there until his death in 1945.

Chapter IV clearly belongs to Snowball. His planning and his actions make him the hero. He is even wounded. But later Napoleon will dispute Snowball's motives and his achievements and paints a very different picture of history. His role in the battle will come up later in the book when the events of history are rewritten by Squealer.

Study Questions

1. How does Mr. Jones spend most of his time after he is kicked off his farm?

2. Who is Mr. Pilkington and how does Orwell describe him?

3. Who is Mr. Frederick and how does Orwell describe him?

4. What is the typical relationship between these two men?

5. How do Foxwood Farm and Pinchfield Farm compare?

6. How do the farmers try to discredit what is happening on Animal Farm?

7. What is the cause of the Battle of the Cowshed?

8. What is Snowball's role in the battle?

9. What part does Boxer play in the battle?

10. What are the results of the Battle of the Cowshed?

Answers

1. After being kicked off his farm, Mr. Jones spends his days at the Red Lion Inn in Willingdon, complaining to anyone who will listen of the injustice that was done to him.

2. Mr. Pilkington is one of Mr. Jones's neighbors. The easygoing gentleman farmer and owner of Foxwood Farm spends his time fishing and hunting.

3. Mr. Frederick is another neighbor and the owner of Pinchfield Farm. He is a tough, shrewd man with a reputation for driving hard bargains and for suing his neighbors.

4. Pilkington and Frederick are on permanently bad terms with each other. They dislike one another so much it is difficult for them to come to any agreement, even in their own best interests.

5. Foxwood is a large, neglected, old-fashioned farm, overgrown by woodland, with worn-out pastures and hedges in a disgraceful condition. Pinchfield Farm is smaller than Foxwood but much better kept.

6. The farmers first laugh at the idea of a farm managed by animals. Then they make up stories about the animals fighting among themselves and torturing each other. They say that the animals on the farm are starving and practicing cannibalism.

7. Stories about the farm from which humans have been expelled circulate among the animals of the neighboring farms. Bulls become savage, sheep break down hedges to eat clover, cows kick over pails, and hunting horses refuse to jump over fences. Fearing more rebellions, the humans join forces with Mr. Jones in an attempt to restore him as the rightful owner.

8. Snowball plans the military strategy. He launches a first wave that seems to retreat in panic. When the humans chase after the animals, Snowball signals the main attack and the humans are defeated. In the battle, Snowball is wounded by a shot from Mr. Jones's gun.

9. Boxer is a terrifying figure, rearing on his hind legs and striking the humans. He injures a stablehand, who later escapes.

10. As a result of the Battle of Cowshed, the humans are driven off in a decisive victory for the animals. Boxer and Snowball are awarded "Animal Hero, First Class" medals for their parts in the battle. A sheep is killed and posthumously awarded an "Animal Hero, Second Class" medal. Mr. Jones's gun is set up under the flagstaff to be fired twice a year: on Midsummer Day, the anniversary of the Rebellion, and on October 12, the anniversary of the Battle of the Cowshed.

Suggested Essay Topics

1. Research the Russian Civil War of 1918-1920. What part did the Allied Forces (Great Britain, France, the United States) and Japan play in this war? How did the foreign invasion of Russia affect the outcome of the war and the Communist Party's rise to power?

2. In Chapter IV we learn that news of the animals' rebellion has spread to neighboring farms, the inhabitants of which are "normal" human characters. They are not surprised by the fact that the animals can talk and reason. Does this make the novel seem more realistic or more fantastical? Does this make it more or less powerful as a political allegory?

Chapter V

New Character:

Minimus: *pig with a remarkable ability for composing songs and poems*

Summary

After the Battle of the Cowshed, Animal Farm is safe from human attack for the time being, due in a large part to Snowball's military genius. However, there remain other problems. Mollie has become more troublesome, working less and becoming more concerned with thoughts of ribbons and sugar. After she is confronted by Clover, Mollie disappears from the farm. Later she is seen by the pigeons when she is pulling a human's cart on the other side of Willingdon. She is never mentioned again. The weather also presents a problem. The winter is bitterly cold, and the pigs make plans for spring planting. Napoleon and Snowball disagree at every point. During their debates, the sheep break into chants of "Four legs good, two legs bad," at the most crucial moments of Snowball's speeches.

Another source of disagreement between the two pigs is the defense of the farm. Snowball wants to stir up rebellions on the other farms by sending more pigeons to sow the seed of revolution. Napoleon wants to fortify from within, securing weapons and training the farm animals.

The biggest controversy stems from Snowball's plans to build a windmill. He paints a picture of a new Animal Farm, powered by electricity produced by the windmill. He promises the animals

heated stalls, modern machinery to make their lives easier, and a three-day work week. Napoleon is completely opposed to his plans, calling instead for increased food production on the farm. The animals are deeply divided on the subject. Only Benjamin believes that nothing will change and that, windmill or not, things will continue to go badly.

On the day of the vote, Napoleon calls the plans for the windmill "nonsense" and advises the animals to vote against it. Snowball, on the other hand, delivers an impassioned speech, painting a picture of Animal Farm as it might be when the animals no longer have to work. Just as the animals are about to vote in favor of the windmill, Napoleon makes a high-pitched sound and nine enormous dogs rush in and chase after Snowball. They are the nine puppies taken from their mothers and secretly raised by Napoleon. The startled Snowball runs for his life and barely escapes through the hedge. He is seen no more.

After Snowball is chased off the farm, Napoleon surrounds himself with the nine dogs, who wag their tails at him the way other dogs had once done to Jones. From the raised platform where Old Major once spoke, Napoleon, with Squealer and Minimus (a pig who has a gift for composing songs and poems) at his side, announces that the Sunday morning meetings will come to an end since they are an unnecessary waste of time. A special committee of pigs will make all the work plans in the future. Some of the animals try to protest and four porkers utter squeals of disapproval, but the growling dogs and the bleating sheep end any chance of discussion. Later, Squealer explains that Napoleon's decision to take on the extra responsibilities of running the farm is to prevent the animals from making "wrong decisions." He hints that Snowball was not a hero, as they all thought, and he says that if the animals don't go along with the new orders, Jones will come back. That makes further protest useless.

Boxer accepts it all without question. He adopts a new maxim, "Napoleon is always right," in addition to his private motto of "I will work harder." Old Major's skull is mounted by the flagstaff, and the animals march past it every Sunday before receiving their work orders for the week from the pigs.

Three weeks later Napoleon announces that work on the wind-

mill will go on as planned. It will take two years. Squealer tells the confused animals that the plans for the windmill were not Snowball's, but actually Napoleon's, and that Napoleon was never really opposed to the windmill. He says that the project will require harder work and reduced rations for all of the animals, except, of course, the pigs.

Analysis

Chapter V begins with the hope of a better future for the animals, but it ends with hopelessness, the termination of the Sunday morning meetings, strict control by a select committee of pigs, and with Napoleon becoming a total dictator. Mollie, dissatisfied with events, cannot accept the new order and the loss of the privileges that she had enjoyed under Jones. She was never really committed to the cause of the Rebellion, and at the first opportunity she escapes, choosing to pull a cart for a human in exchange for ribbons and lump sugar. From a historical perspective, Mollie represents those thousands of Russians who fled their country after the Revolution and during the uncertain years of civil war that followed.

In the early 1920s, while Lenin's health was failing and his leadership faltering, Leon Trotsky and Josef Stalin were in a struggle for control of the Communist party. Those who had the opportunity flooded into Europe and the United States, often leaving behind what wealth they had, satisfied with just saving their lives. Many of these refugees, titled aristocrats under the Tsar, were forced to drive taxis, operate elevators, or open tea rooms to survive.

Benjamin shows his dissatisfaction with the deteriorating conditions on the farm by his cynicism. Although he knows that nothing will change for the animals, unlike Mollie, he chooses to remain where he is and preserve himself by taking the path of least resistance.

Although Napoleon and Snowball disagree on everything, it is the windmill, the modernization and industrialization of Animal Farm, that brings their conflict to a head. For Snowball, who too gets caught up in his own dreams, the windmill is a promise of leisure time for everyone, provided by electrical power that will run the machines and do the hard work presently done by the animals.

Historically, the windmill represents the early attempts after the Revolution to bring Russia into the 20th Century through a series of Five Year Plans. These plans were aimed at building roads, dams, hydroelectric plants and factories, and increasing farm production.

While Snowball focuses on the power of the windmill, Napoleon is concerned with another kind of power, his personal power and control of the farm and the other animals. His ability to achieve his goal of dominance hinges on the dogs. When Napoleon unleashes them and runs Snowball off the farm, he has accomplished two things. He eliminates the competition, and he has at his disposal the enormous power of nine dogs who are blindly faithful only to him. Now, besides the fear that Jones will return, the animals have something more tangible to worry about, the dogs. Any insurrection, protest, or even the slightest disagreement with Napoleon could violently end their lives. The fact that Napoleon performs an about-face on the windmill is easily explained by Squealer, who simply rewrites history. According to Squealer's account, Napoleon was never opposed to the windmill; it was his idea in the first place. And as to the other changes in policy, Squealer easily convinces the animals that the unselfish Napoleon is doing it all for the greater good of the farm. Squealer even begins the campaign of discrediting Snowball's achievements before he was expelled. He tells the animals, "And as to the Battle of the Cowshed, I believe the time will come when we shall find that Snowball's part in it was much exaggerated." The confused and frightened cannot protest. They have no choice but acceptance.

The split between Trotsky and Stalin intensified after the death of Lenin. In a series of political maneuvers, Stalin had Trotsky and his followers expelled from the Communist Party and drove his political enemy into exile. Later, a campaign to discredit Trotsky was launched in the Soviet Union. Trotsky's achievements during the Revolution were erased in a rewriting of Russian history books, and his name remains expunged from Soviet histories to this day. Although Orwell's account of events only depicts Trotsky's exile, the banished Soviet revolutionary spent time organizing supporters in Europe. A brigade of Trotskyites, Orwell among them, fought in the Spanish Civil War against the forces of Francisco Franco. Eventually, Trotsky came to New York where he founded the Communist newspaper the *Daily Worker*. He later fled to Mexico City and was assassinated by an agent of the Soviet Secret Police. In the book, the dogs represent the Secret Police whom Stalin used to crush his political opponents and take total control of the country.

Study Questions

1. Why does Clover confront Mollie?

2. What happens to Mollie?

3. How does Napoleon use the sheep's bleating of "Four legs good, two legs bad" to his advantage?

4. What does Snowball see for the animals as a result of building the windmill?

5. How does Napoleon show his disapproval of Snowball's plans?

6. What is Benjamin's opinion of the windmill?

7. What happens to Snowball?

8. What changes on Animal Farm does Napoleon announce to the animals?

9. How does Squealer explain these changes and Napoleon's intent to build the windmill after all?

10. How does Squealer try to undermine Snowball?

Answers

1. Clover questions Mollie after Mollie is seen standing near the hedge of Foxwood Farm with one of Mr. Pilkington's men stroking her nose. Clover later finds ribbons and sugar hidden in Mollie's stall.

2. Mollie runs away from Animal Farm and the pigeons report seeing her pulling a cart for a human. The animals never mention her again.

3. The sheep begin their bleating whenever Snowball tries to speak at the meetings, and he is unable to get his ideas across to the other animals.

4. Snowball sees the windmill as a source of electric power and heat. He says it will run machinery and do the work now done by the animals. Eventually, the animals' work week would be reduced to three days.

5. Napoleon shows his contempt for the plans by urinating on them.

6. Benjamin doesn't think anything will change for the animals. He says life will go on as it has always gone on—badly.

7. Just as the animals are about to vote against Napoleon and adopt Snowball's plans for the windmill, Napoleon calls in the nine dogs. Snowball, barely getting through the hedge and escaping with his life, is run off the farm.

8. Napoleon, surrounded by the dogs, announces that the Sunday morning meetings are to be abolished as they are no longer necessary. Work schedules for the animals will be decided by a committee of pigs, but there will be no votes. Napoleon also decides to go ahead with plans to build the windmill and warns that this task will require extra work and a cut in the animals' food rations.

9. Squealer convinces the animals that Napoleon was never opposed to the windmill. He further states that the plans were originally Napoleon's. He says Napoleon's actions are called "tactics."

10. Squealer questions Snowball's role in the Battle of the Cowshed. He questions his loyalty and says he expects to find evidence that Snowball's part in the battle was exaggerated.

Suggested Essay Topics

1. Trace the events leading to Napoleon's seizing complete control of the farm, and discuss the different tactics that he uses to succeed.

2. Mollie chooses to live a life of comfortable slavery rather than make the sacrifices necessary in a communal society. Is this

a wise choice? What is the significance of her leaving, both in the world of the novel, and considering that the novel is a political allegory based on actual events?

SECTION TWO

Chapter VI

New Character:

Mr. Whymper: *human solicitor (lawyer) from Willingdon who acts as intermediary between Animal Farm and the outside world*

Summary

Life for the animals begins to get worse. They work harder and longer, 60 hours a week, including Sundays. Boxer is the key to finishing the windmill. He gets up three-quarters of an hour earlier every morning to haul a load of stones from the quarry. Even Benjamin, yolked together with Muriel the goat, does his share. But the routine work on the farm is neglected and shortages develop. One Sunday morning as the animals are waiting to get their orders from the pigs, Napoleon announces that he will begin trade with neighboring farms in order to get money for the supplies they need and for the windmill. Despite food shortages, Napoleon has contracted to sell a stack of hay and some of the wheat crop. If more money is needed, the chickens will have to make a sacrifice and hand over their eggs for sale in Willingdon. The animals are uneasy about the decision, remembering resolutions that were passed against trade with the humans at the first meeting after Jones was expelled. But their weak protest are useless. Objections from the four porkers, who complained when Napoleon abolished the Sunday meetings, are silenced by the growling dogs and the bleating of the sheep. Squealer addresses the animals' concerns regarding the arrangements. He tells them that anti-trade resolutions were never passed at any of the meetings, or even suggested. He blames

the animals' confusion in the matter on lies circulated by Snow-ball. Napoleon employs Mr. Whymper, a solicitor from Willingdon, as his intermediary, and the pigs begin trading with the outside world.

Jones gives up all hope of recovering his farm and fades from the picture. Napoleon, through Whymper, begins negotiations with Pilkington and Frederick, playing one against the other, to close a big deal.

The pigs move into the farmhouse because they are the brains of the farm and need a quiet place to work. Squealer convinces the animals that the farmhouse is more suitable to the dignity of Napoleon whom he calls "Leader." When the animals learn that the pigs are sleeping in beds, Clover thinks she remembers that a commandment directly forbids it. But when Muriel reads what is written on the barn wall, they realize that they are wrong. The commandment says, "No animal shall sleep in a bed with sheets." Squealer easily explains that the warning was never against beds which are just like the animals' stalls, a place to sleep. The commandment is against sheets, a human invention. Once again, Squealer links the pigs' getting special privileges with keeping Jones off the farm.

A violent windstorm knocks down the almost-completed windmill, but Napoleon blames it on Snowball. He declares Snowball an enemy and a traitor and pronounces the death sentence on him. He offers a medal and extra food to the animal who brings Snowball to justice. Any animal's doubts about Snowball melt away when pig footprints are discovered leading in the direction of Foxwood Farm. Napoleon sniffs them and says they are Snowball's. The loss of the windmill will make their already-difficult lives even more difficult, but Napoleon plans to rebuild it at any cost.

Analysis

Orwell's tongue-in-cheek irony is apparent throughout, but especially in the opening lines of Chapter VI:

> All that year the animals worked like slaves. But
> they were happy in their work; they grudged no
> effort or sacrifice, well aware that everything that

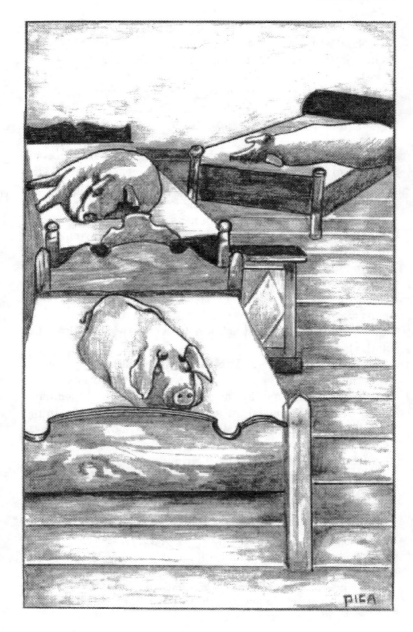

they did was for the benefit of themselves and
those of their kind who would come after them,
and not for a pack of idle, thieving human be-
ings.

The animals are not aware that all of their hard work and their
sacrifices are now benefiting a pack of idle pigs. With Snowball gone
and Napoleon in complete control, the changes on Animal Farm
are coming fast. Building the windmill requires longer hours and
the animals' work week is up to 60 hours. Sunday work is strictly
"voluntary," but any animal who doesn't volunteer has his food rations cut in half. And because of the push to complete the windmill, the farm is neglected. Shortages necessitate trade with
humans which causes another violation of the "unalterable" commandments of Animal Farm. The needs of Napoleon and the farm
afford the lawyer, Whymper, an opportunity for personal gain. The
human, Whymper, represents those opportunists who made the
most of the hardships and famine in Russia in 1921-22 and 1932-
33. Against world opinion and organized efforts to sit back and
watch the Communists starve themselves out of existence, capitalists, including manufacturers in the United States, engaged in
trade with the Soviet Union and made large profits.

Squealer's importance to Napoleon's goals is apparent. He
heads off any animal protest by rewriting history. There was never
a resolution against engaging in trade with the humans. The Fourth
Commandment is aimed at sheets and not beds. He is so convincing when he says, "We have removed the sheets from the farmhouse beds, and sleep between blankets" that no one questions
the fact that blankets are also a human invention. As with the milk
and the apples, the animals are told that the pigs sleeping in beds
is keeping Jones off the farm. Squealer represents propaganda. In
the Soviet Union it was used to influence public opinion, to re-
educate, and to indoctrinate. Even history books were rewritten to
present a more acceptable account of events. And if Squealer's
"logic" fails, there are the growling dogs, ready to use force when it
becomes necessary.

In this chapter Napoleon makes Snowball the "scapegoat" for
all the problems on Animal Farm. A scapegoat is a person or group

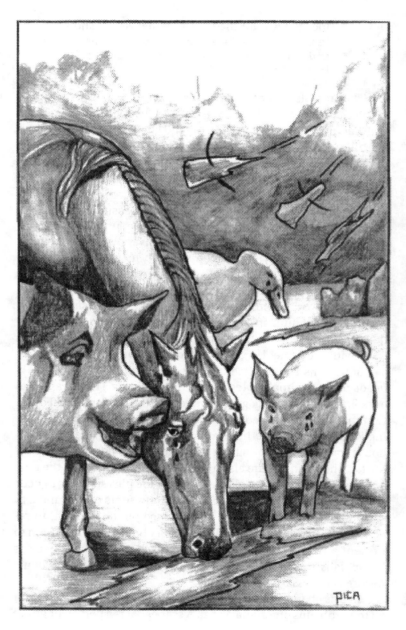

that is blamed for whatever goes wrong in a society. Finding a scapegoat focuses attention away from the real problem, and it unifies the energies of a society against a common enemy and what they perceive to be the cause of all their suffering. In *Animal Farm* this is Snowball. Squealer attributes the animals' confusion regarding trade with the humans to Snowball's lies. In actuality, the windmill is blown down because of faulty plans; the walls are too thin. Since Napoleon took credit for the plans, he should be blamed for the disaster. But by shifting the guilt and making Snowball the villain, Napoleon appears blameless, and Snowball becomes a traitor and an enemy of Animal Farm.

Study Questions

1. How did the lives of the animals become more difficult in the beginning of Chapter VI?

2. How does Boxer deal with these new difficulties?

3. How do conditions on the farm under Napoleon's leadership compare to when Jones was the owner?

4. Who is Mr. Whymper and why does he come to the farm?

5. How does Squealer address the animals' concerns about engaging in trade with the humans?

6. What change occurs to the living conditions of the pigs?

7. What happens to the Fourth Commandment?

8. How does Squealer answer their questions concerning the Fourth Commandment?

9. What happens to the windmill?

10. What does Napoleon say happened to the windmill, and what does he do?

Answers

1. The animals have to work a 60 hour week, including Sundays, or their food rations are cut in half. The harvest is less successful, and gathering stones for the windmill is hard work.

2. Boxer makes arrangements to get up three-quarters of an hour earlier so he can go to the quarry to collect a load of broken stone for the windmill. His two slogans, "Napoleon is always right" and "I will work harder," help him to deal with the hardships.

3. In the summer, conditions were about the same. They had no more food, but they had no less. Later, there were some shortages, including paraffin oil, nails, string, dog biscuits, and iron for the horses' shoes. There was also a need to buy seed and fertilizer, and tools and machinery for the windmill.

4. When Napoleon decides to trade with the humans, Mr. Whymper agrees to act as Napoleon's agent to secure the necessary supplies. Whymper sees it as an opportunity to make a large profit for himself.

5. Squealer assures them that a resolution against engaging in trade and using money was never passed or even suggested. There is no proof it ever existed because it is not written down. He says the whole problem can be traced to lies circulated by Snowball.

6. The pigs move into the farmhouse and begin sleeping in beds.

7. When Clover asks Muriel to read the commandment, it has been changed. It now says, "No animal shall sleep in a bed with sheets."

8. Squealer says that the commandment wasn't against beds. It was against sheets which are a human invention. Therefore, the pigs have removed the sheets and sleep on blankets. He adds the warning that Jones will come back if the pigs don't sleep on beds.

9. Because the walls were built too thin, the windmill blows down during a violent storm.

10. Napoleon blames the absent Snowball for knocking down the windmill. He pronounces the death sentence on Snowball and offers an "Animal Hero, Second Class" and half a

bushel of apples to the animal that brings Snowball to justice.

Suggested Essay Topics

1. It has become evident in this chapter that all of the animals are not equal, and life on the farm is settling into familiar hierarchies and oppressions. What do you think this says about Orwell's beliefs about human nature? Could this happen in our society?

2. In Chapter VI Squealer plays a most important role in Napoleon's push to become the dictator of Animal Farm. What does Squealer do to enable Napoleon to achieve this goal? What was the significance of propaganda, the management of information and the alteration of history, in Stalin's rise to power?

Chapter VII

Summary

It is bitter winter and the food is in short supply. Corn rations are cut and much of the potato crop is spoiled by the frost. Starvation stares animals in the face. To conceal their hardships from the outside world, Napoleon tricks Whymper on his weekly visits to the farm into believing the farm is prospering. In Whymper's hearing, the sheep talk about an increase in their rations. Empty food bins are filled with sand and topped with meal to give him the impression that there is an abundance of food.

During this time Napoleon is rarely seen by the animals, even on Sunday mornings, and when he does come out of the farmhouse, he is surrounded by six fierce dogs.

In January, with conditions growing worse, Squealer announces that the hens must surrender their eggs for sale. Napoleon and Whymper have entered into an agreement to sell 400 eggs a week. The hens object, calling the sale of their eggs murder, and three Black Minorca pullets lead a rebellion against Napoleon's orders. They lay their eggs in the rafters and smash them to the floor rather than turn them over for sale. Napoleon cuts off their rations and decrees that any animal who gives them even one grain of corn will be put to death. The hens hold out for five days but then give in and surrender their eggs. Each week Whymper comes to collect 400 eggs as agreed.

Frederick and Pilkington are anxious to buy a pile of timber that had been cut and stacked 10 years earlier. When negotiations are going well with one farmer, a rumor is circulated around the

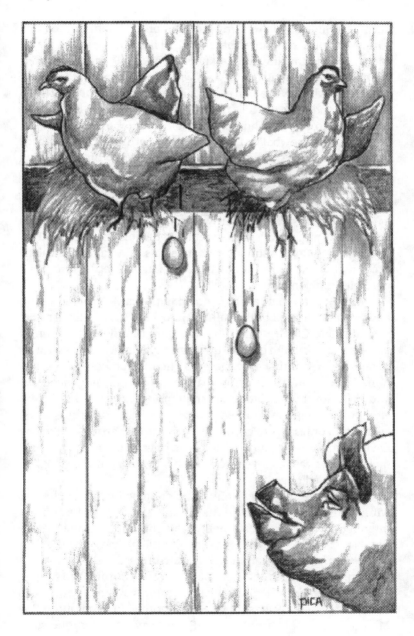

farm that Snowball is working with the other. Then, in the early spring, the pigs announce that Snowball is coming onto the farm each night and causing trouble, knocking over milk pails and breaking eggs. Whenever anything goes wrong on the farm, it is attributed to Snowball. Napoleon calls for an investigation of Snowball's activities, and Squealer tells the frightened animals that Snowball is planning to guide the humans in another attack on Animal Farm. Squealer calls Snowball a traitor to Animal Farm and a secret agent of Mr. Jones. He says that Snowball was prevented from turning the farm over to Jones during the Battle of the Cowshed by Napoleon's bravery. When Boxer questions Squealer's account of the events, he is told, "Our Leader, Comrade Napoleon…has stated categorically…that Snowball was Jones's agent from the very beginning…and from long before the Rebellion was ever thought of." Although Boxer ultimately changes his mind after Squealer's account, Squealer eyes him with suspicion and regards him as a possible troublemaker.

When the animals are assembled in the yard, Napoleon, who has awarded himself both "Animal Hero, First Class" and "Animal Hero, Second Class" medals, has the dogs round up the animals who have caused him problems. These include the three hens who organized the mutiny over the eggs, the four porkers who questioned Napoleon's decision to end the Sunday morning meetings, and even Boxer who comes under attack by the dogs. But Boxer's strength is too much and he fights off the dogs. The others, however, after confessing to crimes against Animal Farm, are killed by having their throats ripped out by the dogs. More and more animals step forward to reveal plots with Snowball, only to be killed by the frenzied dogs.

Clover, like the other animals, is confused by what she has witnessed. She is sure that events are not unfolding as the animals intended when Jones was expelled, but she will continue to support Napoleon. As bad as things are, she still believes that the lives of the animals are better than they were under Jones.

In the final pages of the chapter, Napoleon forbids the singing of *Beasts of England* because the revolution is over and the song is no longer necessary. It is replaced by another song composed by Minimus: "Animal Farm, Animal Farm,/Never through me shalt thou come to harm!"

Analysis

Napoleon's brutality is the major focus of this chapter. Conditions grow worse as a result of bad weather and poor planning, and the animals are called upon to make more sacrifices. The hens refuse to turn over their eggs for sale because it is the equivalent of murdering their unborn clutches. For the first time there is indication of another revolution on the farm. But Napoleon, using the dogs, ruthlessly starves them out. Nine hens are killed in the process of imposing his will. Historically, the Mutiny of the Hens represents the reaction of large numbers of Russian peasants who rebelled against Stalin's First Five-Year Plan. They chose to burn their crops and slaughter their livestock in a time of famine, rather than turn them over for sale to foreign countries.

No one was safe on Animal Farm. Even the loyal and faithful Boxer comes under suspicion and attack when he questions Squealer's latest allegations against Snowball. Most brutal is the scene of confessions and murder. Conveniently, all of Napoleon's "enemies" publicly admit their crimes and are executed. It might appear implausible that animals who didn't engage in these activities would confess, knowing they were to be killed. The story is an allegory, and Orwell is portraying the "Great Purge of 1937-38," a time when Stalin cleared out suspected enemies from the government. In public trials, prominent Russian leaders made public confessions to "crimes against the state." Many of the confessions were forced by threats against family members or torture. Later the "guilty" were exiled to labor camps or executed. The casualties of Stalin's purges during this time have been estimated in the hundreds of thousands.

Interestingly, in this chapter, Orwell deviates from his impersonal third-person narrative point of view, which relates events without commentary or emotion. For the first time, he takes the reader into the mind of one of the characters. After the murders, the reader is given insight into Clover's feelings, and through Clover, into the minds and the thoughts of the other animals. Clover is confused and afraid but lacks the ability to convey her feelings to the others. In her heart she still believes that she is better off under Napoleon than under Jones. The causes for her inaction are her ignorance, inertia, and fear. This best explains why the animals on Animal Farm never resist, and perhaps it explains why the Russian people never rebelled against Stalin, the man who subverted their revolution.

Study Questions

1. How do the animals plan to prevent the second windmill from being destroyed?

2. Besides the work on the windmill, what other hardships do the animals have to face in Chapter VII?

3. How does Napoleon hope to prevent the outside world from finding out about the food shortages on Animal Farm?

4. What is the cause of concern among the chickens?

5. How do the hens react to Napoleon's news about the eggs?

6. How does Napoleon deal with the Mutiny of the Hens and what are the results?

7. Besides the destruction of the windmill, for what other things is Snowball blamed?

8. What "news" does Squealer reveal about Snowball and the Battle of the Cowshed, and what is Boxer's reaction?

9. What happens at the assembly of the animals in the yard?

10. What is Clover's reaction to the violent events?

Answers

1. They plan to make the walls three feet thick, which means more stone is needed and more work is required of them.

2. The winter is bitter cold and food is in short supply. The animals' corn ration is drastically cut and the frost spoils the greater part of the potato crop.

3. Napoleon uses Whymper to spread the word that the animals are prospering. He does this by filling the almost empty bins with sand and covering it with grain and meal. He has the sheep remark in Whymper's hearing that food rations have been increased, and Whymper is fooled.

4. Napoleon accepts a contract, through Whymper, to sell 400 eggs a week. The money from the sale would buy enough grain to get the farm through the winter. The hens, ready to hatch clutches of chicks, say taking the eggs would be murder.

5. The hens lay their eggs in the rafters of the barn, choosing to smash them to the ground rather than turn them over to Napoleon for sale.

6. Napoleon orders the hens' rations stopped and death to any animal who gives them even one grain of corn. The hens hold out for five days and then give in. Nine hens die in the mutiny and are buried in the orchard. Napoleon delivers four 400 a week for sale as contracted.

7. He is blamed for stealing corn, upsetting milk pails, breaking eggs, trampling seedbeds, gnawing the bark on fruit trees, breaking windows, blocking up drains, stealing the key to the storage shed, milking the cows while they sleep, and inciting the rats to cause trouble.

8. Squealer says that documents have been recently found that prove Snowball was Jones's secret agent, and that he planned to turn over the farm to the humans during a critical part of the battle. Boxer says he doesn't believe it, although he changes his mind when Squealer indicates that Napoleon has stated categorically that Snowball was a traitor from the beginning.

9. At a signal from Napoleon, the dogs drag the four porkers who protested Napoleon's plan to stop the Sunday meetings into the yard. They are followed by the three hens who were the leaders of the rebellion over the eggs, a goose, and three sheep. After confessing to crimes against Animal Farm, their throats are torn out by the dogs. Three dogs attack Boxer, but he is too strong and fights them off. The confessions continue until there is a pile of corpses lying at Napoleon's feet.

10. Clover knows that the scenes of terror and slaughter are not what they looked forward to when Old Major stirred them to overthrow man. They had envisioned an animal society

with no whips, no hunger, no inequality, where all worked according to their abilities, and the strong protected the weak. But she doesn't have the words to express her thoughts, and she has no desire to rebel because she believes their lives are still better under Napoleon's rule.

Suggested Essay Topics

1. The murders and purges which occur in Chapter VII are brutal and terrifying, yet the animals are quick to forget about them and to accept explanations. Explain how the pigs can make words appear more real than the actual murders. How does this have frightening applications in reality, both historically and today?

2. Clover seems to be the only animal to suspect that things on Animal Farm aren't the way they had planned. Why doesn't she communicate her suspicions to the others? Why doesn't she consider a rebellion and why is she still willing to follow Napoleon?

Chapter VIII

Summary

After the terror of the executions dies down, Clover, recalling that the Sixth Commandment forbade killing, asks Muriel to read what is written on the barn. The Commandment clearly states, "No animal shall kill another animal *without cause*."

Work on the second windmill goes on, along with the regular work of the farm. To the animals it seems as if they are working harder and being fed less than when they worked for Jones. Every Sunday Squealer reads from a long list of figures that prove how production is increasing, but the animals would prefer fewer figures and more food.

Napoleon appears in public less and less often, and when he does, it is always with his dogs. A black cockerel marches in front of him and cock-a-doodle-doos before Napoleon speaks. The animals refer to him formally as "our Leader, Comrade Napoleon," "Father of All Animals," "Terror of Mankind," "Protector of the Sheep-fold," and "Ducklings' Friend." Minimus, the pig, even composes a poem in Napoleon's honor, which is inscribed on the barn wall opposite the Seven Commandments.

Through Whymper, negotiations for the sale of the pile of timber continue with Pilkington and Frederick. Rumors are renewed that Snowball is working with Frederick, and that they have plans to invade Animal Farm and blow up the windmill. Three chickens confess to conspiring with Snowball in a plot to murder Napoleon. The chickens are quickly executed and precautions are taken for their leader's safety. Snowball is blamed for mixing weeds with the wheat crop. The animals learn that he never received the "Animal Hero, First Class" medal after the Battle of the Cowshed; it was merely a legend spread by Snowball himself.

As relations with Frederick grow worse, relations with Pilkington become almost friendly. The pigeons, who were still sent out to spread "tidings of the Rebellion," are forbidden to set foot on Foxwood Farm and concentrate on Pinchfield Farm. They are ordered to drop their former slogan of "Death to Humanity" in favor of "Death to Frederick."

In the autumn, the windmill is completed and the animals are proud of their achievement. Napoleon announces that it will be called "Napoleon Mill." Two days later he tells the assembled animals that the woodpile has been sold to Frederick and that all relations with Foxwood Farm have been broken off. The slogan "Death to Pilkington" replaces "Death to Frederick." The animals are told that the rumors (spread by Snowball) about an attack by Frederick were false. Payment for the timber, in five pound notes, would be enough to buy the machinery for the new windmill. At a special meeting, the animals file slowly past the pile of money as Napoleon, wearing both his decorations reposes on a bed of straw on the platform. Their procession is almost religious in nature— worship of the bank notes. But three days after Frederick's men remove the wood, Whymper brings word to Napoleon that the bank notes are forgeries and that Frederick has stolen the wood.

The next morning Frederick and his men, armed with half a dozen guns, attack the farm. Many animals are wounded and others hide in the farm buildings. Napoleon sends a message to Pilkington begging for help, but his response is, "Serves you right." As the frightened animals watch, Frederick packs blasting powder into the base of the windmill and blows it up. The animals' fear turns to rage and they attack the humans, driving them off the farm, though at great cost. Even Napoleon's tail is wounded. All traces of the windmill are gone, and the blast has scattered the stones and all their hard work. Squealer proclaims the event a great victory for the animals, and the gun is fired to celebrate the Battle of the Windmill, as the "victory" is called.

A few days later the pigs discover a case of whisky in the cellar of the farmhouse. That night there are strange sounds of singing

and celebrating. Napoleon, wearing Jones's bowler hat, is seen galloping around the yard. The next morning, when Squealer makes his appearance at nine o'clock, he tells the assembled animals that Napoleon is dying, that Snowball put poison in his food. At eleven o'clock Napoleon pronounces the death sentence on anyone who drinks alcohol. But in the evening, when he is better, he sends Whymper into town to get books on brewing and distilling alcohol.

One night Squealer is found with an overturned paint pot and a paint brush at the foot of a broken ladder near the wall of the barn. The dogs escort him quickly back into the farmhouse. When the animals, who vaguely remember a Commandment about drinking, check the barn, the Fifth Commandment now reads, "No animal shall drink alcohol *to excess.*"

Analysis

Historically, the chapter deals with Hitler's rise to power in Nazi Germany in the 1930s and the early years leading up to the beginning of World War II. The animals' one success in the face of overwhelming hardships, the completion of the second windmill, is short-lived. After he lulls Napoleon into a false sense of security, Frederick succeeds in stealing the woodpile by paying for it with forged bank notes. Frederick adds insult to injury when he and his men invade Animal Farm. The animals' sacrifice has been for nothing as they watch the blast of dynamite destroy the windmill and scatter all of their hard work. The agreement between Napoleon and Frederick for the sale of the woodpile suggests the Stalin-Hitler Pact signed in 1939. This political alliance of two dictators, Hitler and Stalin, alarmed Europe and the United States. It enabled Germany to expand its territory by dividing parts of Central Europe with the Soviets. The pact secured Hitler's eastern border, allowing him to turn his attention to Western Europe and begin what would become World War II. After a series of German successes in Poland, France, and the British Army's retreat from Dunkirk, Germany invaded Russia in 1941. This is represented by the Battle of the Windmill. The forged bank notes are Orwell's way of satirizing the worthless treaty. Hitler's Russian Campaign was at first successful as the highly mechanized German Army fought to within miles of

Moscow. But the determination of the Soviet people and the severity of the Russian winter slowed and eventually stopped the invasion. The war on the Russian Front was responsible for millions of Russian casualties. Published reports indicated that the fighting was so fierce, hardly a family was spared. It is something Orwell alludes to when he says, "Even Napoleon, who was directing operations from the rear, had the tip of his tail chipped by a pellet." But Squealer is able to turn even the terrible defeat at the Battle of the Windmill into victory by simply proclaiming it so.

In addition to the battle, the chapter focuses on the changes that continue to occur on the farm. After the terror of the purges, the animals think they remember that the Sixth Commandment expressly forbids one animal killing another. It was a point emphasized by Old Major when he first addressed the animals. But when Muriel reads what is written on the barn, the animals realize that they are again mistaken. Killing is permitted for the right reasons, and Napoleon can determine what those reasons are. Once again Squealer has succeeded in changing history. There are other changes too, as the animals have come to regard Napoleon, their new "master" much in the same way they once regarded Jones. Napoleon is distant and aloof, even inhabiting a separate apartment from the rest of the pigs in the farmhouse. He takes his meals alone, eating off fine china, with two dogs in waiting. He never associates with the "lower" animals. As his newly created titles suggest, he has grown far above any of the other animals on the farm. Napoleon rarely appears in public, but when he does, he is protected by his dogs who have become his personal bodyguards.

The campaign to malign Snowball's reputation picks up momentum, and it now appears that things are even worse than any of the animals could imagine. Squealer reports that recently discovered documents reveal that the hero of the Battle of the Cowshed isn't a hero at all. Snowball is proclaimed a traitor against Animal Farm, in league with the humans from the beginning. Even now, Squealer assures the animals, Snowball is preparing to lead another human attack on the farm.

When the pigs discover alcohol, another step is taken in their journey to become more and more like man. At first the negative effects of consuming a case of whiskey make Napoleon sick. But when he recovers from his hangover, his attentions turn toward producing his own alcohol. The field, once intended as a grazing ground for retired animals, is to be sown with barley for the pigs' beer. Thus, another of the "unalterable" commandments has been changed to suit Napoleon.

Study Questions

1. How does the Sixth Commandment change?

2. What are the titles invented for Napoleon?

3. What happens when Minimus composes the poem "Comrade Napoleon"?

4. What other confessions are made by animals in this chapter and what are the results?

5. What is the latest information Squealer reveals to the animals about Snowball?

6. What does Napoleon do with the woodpile?

7. How does Frederick cheat Napoleon?

8. What happens in the Battle of the Windmill?

9. Why does Squealer tell the animals that Napoleon is dying?

10. How is the Fifth Commandment changed?

Answers

1. The commandment becomes "No animal shall kill any other animal *without cause.*"

2. The pigs call him "Father of All Animals," "Terror of Mankind," "Protector of the Sheep-fold," and "Ducklings' Friend."

3. Napoleon approves of the poem and orders that it be inscribed on the barn wall opposite the commandments.

4. Three hens confess to entering into a plot with Snowball to murder Napoleon. A gander confesses to working with Snowball to put weeds in the corn seed. The hens are executed, and the gander promptly commits suicide. Later, a pig is assigned the job of tasting all of Napoleon's food to see if it is poisoned.

5. Squealer tells the animals that Snowball never received a medal after the Battle of the Cowshed. He says that Snowball is working with the humans to plan another attack on the farm.

6. He contracts with Frederick to sell the wood in exchange for bank notes. The money is to be used to buy necessary provisions.

7. Frederick pays for the woodpile with counterfeit money. In effect, he steals the wood.

8. Frederick and his men invade the farm. Many animals are killed or wounded, and before being driven off, Frederick blows up the rebuilt windmill.

9. Napoleon is sick from drinking too much alcohol. The rumor is that Snowball has poisoned his food.

10. The commandment becomes, "No animal shall drink alcohol *to excess.*"

Suggested Essay Topics

1. Research Hitler's rise to power in Germany in the 1930s and compare it to Stalin's rise to power in Russia in the 1930s.

2. The theme of deception is prevalent in this chapter. Napoleon is tricked with phony bank notes. What qualities in the animals make them vulnerable to deception? Which "human vices" does deception utilize?

SECTION TWO

Chapter IX

Summary

Work begins on rebuilding the windmill. Boxer, injured in the Battle of the Windmill, refuses to take even a day off from work. Clover and Benjamin are concerned about his failing health. Boxer's hope is that he can see the windmill well under way before his retirement. Although when the Rebellion first occurred there were plans to retire the animals, as yet, no animal had actually retired. The pasture, originally set aside for this purpose, is now being used to grow barley for the pigs.

Winter is severe and the rations are reduced, except for the pigs and the dogs. Squealer calls it a "readjustment." He tells the hungry animals that reducing everyone's rations would be against the fundamental principles of Animalism. He proves to them logically, by reading out a list of figures, that these is no food shortage, and that their lives are better than they ever were under Jones. But the memory of Jones has faded from their minds. There is an increase in the population among the pigs on the farm, and it is apparent that Napoleon, the only boar on the farm, is the sire. Plans are made to build a school to educate them. It becomes a rule that when any animal meets a pig on the path, they must step aside in deference to the pig. Rations, "readjusted" in December, are reduced again in February, and the pigs begin brewing their own beer.

To make up for the hardships, there are more songs, more speeches and more parades, which are called "Spontaneous Demonstrations." The pigs lead the others around the farm carrying banners in honor of Napoleon.

In April the farm is proclaimed a Republic and Napoleon is elected president. On the same day, Squealer tells the animals that documents have been found that link Snowball and Jones from the beginning, and prove that Snowball openly fought on Jones's side. In fact, according to the documents, Snowball was the leader of the human forces and had led a charge against the animals with the words, "Long live Humanity!"

Moses, the raven, returns to Animal Farm with his tales about Sugarcandy Mountain, which he tells to the starving, overworked animals. His visions of the place where they will go when they die keep the believing animals happy. Although the pigs declare his stories to be lies, they allow him to remain without working, and they give him an allowance of beer every day.

Boxer's lung collapses while he is working on the windmill. Benjamin hopes that he and Boxer will both be allowed to retire and spend their last days as companions. Squealer convinces the concerned animals that Boxer will be treated in the hospital in Willingdon, and for two days Boxer remains in his stall, taking medicine found in the farmhouse. When a horse cart comes to remove Boxer, Benjamin, who can read as well as any of the pigs, reads the sign on the cart to the assembled animals. "Alfred Simmonds, Horse Slaughterer and Glue Boiler, Willingdon, Dealer in Hides and Bone-Meal. Kennels Supplied." The animals alert Boxer, but in his weakened state, he cannot escape; he is carried off the farm and never seen again. Three days later it is announced that Boxer died in the hospital after receiving the best care. Squealer's account of Boxer's last hours, and his explanation about the cart, allay the animals' concerns. He says that it had once be-longed to the knacker, but was bought by the veterinary surgeon who had not yet had time to paint over the old name. A wreath of laurels from the garden is sent to be laid on Boxer's grave, and the pigs plan a private memorial service for their fallen comrade. The animals are glad that Boxer died happy. On the day of the banquet, a grocer's van delivers another crate of whiskey to the farmhouse and the pigs celebrate.

Analysis

This is the climactic chapter in the novel. It is here, more than

in any place, that the Old Major's dream of the revolution is betrayed. The ideals of the Rebellion are a dim memory for most of the animals, and the living conditions under Jones have all but faded from their minds. Napoleon and the pigs have established themselves as the new aristocracy, and have decorated themselves with ribbons. The once-hoped-for utopian society has given way to new elitism. Pigs are the new masters, and when an animal passes a pig, the animal must stand aside. There are more pigs, Napoleon's children, to be raised apart and educated in the new school that the other animals will build for them. Even the memory of Snowball, the hero of the Battle of the Cowshed, is gone, replaced by the image of a coward and a traitor, who fought against the animals and was stopped only by Napoleon's bravery.

There are a few diversions to keep the animals' minds off their troubles. The pigs stage "Spontaneous Demonstrations" filled with parades and songs and poems to commemorate Napoleon's glories. And there is Moses, who returns to the farm with his stories of Sugarcandy Mountain. Like the Russian Orthodox Church, which was ridiculed and persecuted after the Communist Revolution, Moses had been chased from the farm. But when living conditions grow worse, he is allowed back in to instill in the starving animals the hope for an afterlife, and to keep them more manageable in this life. Karl Marx called religion the opiate of the people, and Stalin used the reopened churches, filled with secret police and government agents, to soothe the frustrations of the peasants, and as a source of information.

It is the sale of Boxer to the knacker that reveals how evil Napoleon has become. In Chapter I, Old Major predicts that Jones will sell out even the loyal Boxer when he is no longer productive; but it is Napoleon who fulfills the prophecy. Boxer, Napoleon's greatest supporter, the farm's hardest and most faithful worker, the hero of the Battle of the Cowshed, and the main force in the building and rebuilding of the windmill, is sold for enough money to buy the pigs a case of whiskey. The revolution is over, its ideals betrayed by Napoleon and the pigs.

Study Questions

1. What is Boxer's ambition after the Battle of the Windmill?

2. How do the animals' lives become harder after the windmill is blown up?

3. How does Squealer convince them that their lives are better?

4. What is a "Spontaneous Demonstration"?

5. What new information does Squealer reveal about Snowball?

6. What purpose does Moses the raven's return to the farm serve?

7. How do the pigs react to Moses' return?

8. What happens to Boxer?

9. How does Squealer explain the events surrounding Boxer's removal from the farm and his death?

10. Where do the pigs get the money to buy whiskey for their banquet?

Answers

1. Boxer hopes to see the work on rebuilding the windmill get well underway before he reaches the age of retirement.

2. The winter is severe. Their rations are reduced, and they must rebuild the windmill as well as do their work on the farm. The contract for the sale of eggs is increased to 600. Lanterns are removed from their stalls to save oil.

3. Squealer produces lists and figures indicating they have more oats, hay, and turnips than they did under Jones. He tells them that they work shorter hours, their drinking water is better, and more of their young survive infancy. They have more straw in their stalls, and they have fewer fleas.

4. At an appointed time the animals, led by the pigs, would leave work and march around the farm in military formation. Clover and Boxer carry a green banner with the slogan, "Long live Comrade Napoleon!" Later there are songs and poems in Napoleon's honor. It helps the animals forget their empty bellies.

5. Squealer has documents to prove that Snowball was not only in league with Jones, but that he led the attack against the animals at the Battle of the Cowshed. He says that the wounds on Snowball's back were inflicted by Napoleon's teeth.

6. Moses tells the animals about Sugarcandy Mountain, a place where they will go when they die. It is a place where they will have rest and food. His stories help keep the animals happy.

7. They all declare his stories about Sugarcandy Mountain are lies, but they permit him to remain on the farm and not work. They also give him an allowance of beer every day.

8. When Boxer's lung collapses and he is no longer able to work, Napoleon sends him to the horse slaughterer in Willingdon.

9. Squealer tells the animals that Boxer died in the hospital after receiving the best treatment. He says the wagon, which took Boxer, was once owned by the knacker and bought by the veterinary surgeon, who didn't have a chance to paint over the old name.

10. They got the money from the sale of Boxer to the knacker.

Suggested Essay Topics

1. Old Major's view of the future was a bleak one for the animals under Jones. He even predicted that Boxer would be sold to the knacker. His dream was for a utopian society without man and his evil ways. Discuss Old Major's view of the future and show how and why he was both correct and mistaken in his thinking. How does this relate to historical events?

2. Boxer's cruel death is a result of Napoleon's tyrannical rule. Although some of the animals are smart enough to recognize that they are living under tyranny, they do not act. Do you think Orwell is passing judgement on the animals for not trying to change their situation? Does knowledge of a crime not coupled with action constitute complicity in the crime?

Chapter X

Summary

Years pass and most of the old animals who fought in the Rebellion are gone. Muriel, Bluebell, Jessie, and Pincher are dead, and so is Mr. Jones. Snowball is forgotten, and Boxer is forgotten. Only Benjamin is much the same, only older, sadder, and more quiet. The young animals possess none of the ideals that inspired the Rebellion. They accept everything that they are told about the Rebellion and the principles of Animalism without question. The farm is more prosperous, enlarged by two fields bought from Mr. Pilkington. Mr. Whymper has made a handsome profit from his work as Napoleon's agent. The completed windmill has never provided the luxuries promised by Snowball. It is used instead for milling corn, which brings in a handsome profit for the pigs. The lives of the animals have become even harder. They are hungry most of the time. They sleep on straw, labor in the fields, and drink from the pool. In the winter they are cold, and in the summer they are bothered by flies. But Squealer's endless list of figures indicates that their lives are better. It's good to be a pig, and there are more of them. They are the administrators who insure the working of the farm. They make countless files, reports, minutes, and memoranda on large pieces of paper which they burn as soon as they are filled. But the animals haven't given up hope. The Republic of the Animals, which Old Major had foretold, is still believed.

In early summer, Squealer takes the sheep to an isolated part of the farm where they remain for a whole week. It is just after their return that the animals see the pigs, including Napoleon, who is

holding a whip in his trotter, walking around the farm on two legs. Just as some animals were about to utter some protest, the sheep break into a loud bleating of "Four legs good, two legs *better!*" When Clover and Benjamin go to the barn to see if the Seven Commandments have changed, Benjamin, for the first time consents to read what is printed on the wall. There is only one commandment which says, "ALL ANIMALS ARE EQUAL BUT SOME ANIMALS ARE MORE EQUAL THAN OTHERS."

After this the pigs buy a wireless radio, a telephone, and subscriptions to newspapers, and they begin wearing clothes from Mr. Jones's wardrobe.

A week later a deputation of neighboring farmers is invited to tour the farm. In the evening the humans and the pigs are seated around a long table drinking and playing a friendly game of cards. Mr. Pilkington proposes a toast to a new era of trust and cooperation between Animal Farm and it's human neighbors. The animals work harder and receive less food than any animals in the county, and Mr. Pilkington is impressed by this. He plans to introduce on his own farm many of the practices he has witnessed there. He ends with the words, "To the prosperity of Animal Farm." Before returning the toast, Napoleon makes some minor corrections. He announces that the animals will no longer refer to one another as comrade, the boar's skull nailed to the post in the garden has been buried, and the green flag has been changed by removing the hoof and horn. He tells them that the name of the farm has been changed back to "The Manor Farm," its correct and original name, and that he looks forward to a future of trust and friendship with his human neighbors, Napoleon's toast is, "To the prosperity of The Manor Farm!" After the cheers, they resume their card game.

The confused animals, who have been watching it all through the window, slip quietly away. But before they go 20 yards, they hear a great uproar from the farmhouse. Rushing back, they see a violent quarrel in progress. The trouble stems from Napoleon and Pilkington simultaneously playing an ace of spades. As the animals look from man to pig, they can see no difference between the faces of the humans and the faces of the pigs.

Analysis

With the passage of time, many of those who fought in the Rebellion are dead and forgotten. The new animals have only a dim tradition passed on by word of mouth. The memories of the older animals have been so altered by Squealer's revisions of history that it is impossible to know what is real.

With the prosperity of Animal Farm, only the pigs and the dogs have flourished. But the naive animals still have faith they will be part of the great Animal Republic Old Major once promised. Even when the pigs begin walking on two legs, there can be no protest. The sheep's new slogan (Or is it the slogan they always bleated? The animals can't remember.) convinces them that walking on two legs has always been preferable to walking on four.

The final example of Squealer's "double speak" can be seen when the Seven Commandments are changed into one. Of course all animals are equal. But the pigs are more equal than the others. They are now the masters who carry the whips and live in the house and wear clothes. They have become the new aristocracy. Equality equals inequality.

Orwell's final irony is witnessed when the humans come to visit the farm. They openly refer to the farm animals as "lower" animals, and they observe them working harder and longer for less food than any other animals in the county. The changes announced by Napoleon to Pilkington, their pledges of trust, and talk of a new era of understanding between Animal Farm and its neighbors serve to show that there is now little difference between pig and man. This forced friendship is Orwell's way of showing the uneasy alliance between Russia and the Allies after the 1941 invasion of the Soviet Union by Germany. Great Britain, France, and the United States may have been fighting on the same side with Stalin and the Soviets, but there was no trust. Ironically, the words of their toast are hardly finished when someone cheats in the card game. The animals looking in the window cannot tell the difference between the men and the pigs. They no longer need to fear that Jones will come back to make their difficult lives miserable; he has already come back in the form of Napoleon and the pigs.

Study Questions

1. What happens to Mr. Jones?

2. How does the farm prosper in the years after Boxer's death?

3. What kind of work do the pigs do on the now-prosperous farm?

4. What is the new slogan learned by the sheep and why?

5. What happens to the Seven Commandments?

6. What modern conveniences do the pigs enjoy after they learn to walk on two legs?

7. What observations has Mr. Pilkington made on his tour of Animal Farm?

8. What changes does Napoleon announce at his meeting with the humans?

9. What causes the fight between Napoleon and Pilkington?

10. What happens as the animals look into the farmhouse window, and what does it mean?

Answers

1. Mr. Jones died in an inebriate's home in another part of the country.

2. It is enlarged by two fields bought from Mr. Pilkington, and threshing machine, hay elevator, and new buildings are added. The windmill is successfully completed, and it is used for milling corn, which brings in a handsome profit.

3. The pigs are involved in the endless work of supervision and organization, work the other animals are too ignorant to understand. They fill up large sheets of papers with writing, and as soon as they are so covered, they burn them in the furnace.

4. When the pigs learn to walk on two legs, the sheep learn a new slogan, "Four legs good, two legs *better!*"

5. They are replaced by a single commandment, "All animals are equal, but some animals are more equal than others."

6.   The pigs buy themselves a wireless radio and make plans to install a telephone. They take out subscriptions to newspapers and begin wearing clothes found in Mr. Jones's closet.

7.   Mr. Pilkington has seen that the animals under the supervision of the pigs work harder and eat less than any animals in the county. He plans to use some of the practices he has seen on his own farm.

8.   He says the animals will no longer refer to each other as "comrade." Old Major's skull, nailed to a post in the garden, has been buried, and the hoof and horn on the flag have been removed. He also says that the name of the farm has been changed back to "The Manor Farm."

9.   They both play an ace of spades at the same time. Someone is cheating.

10. The animals can't tell the difference between the pigs and the humans. Napoleon has become just like Mr. Jones whom he has replaced.

Suggested Essay Topics

1.   Compare Manor Farm at the beginning of the story with Manor Farm in the last chapter. What changes have taken place and what things have remained the same? What, in your opinion, is better for the animals and why?

2.   Assume that Napoleon was the pig exiled from Animal Farm, and that Snowball became its leader. With your knowledge of Snowball's ideals and beliefs, discuss how you think the animals would have done under his leadership. What do you think would have been different and why?

Sample Analytical Paper Topics

The following paper topics are designed to test your understanding of the novel as a whole and to analyze important themes and literary devices. Following each question is a sample outline to help get you started.

Topic #1

"Power tends to corrupt and absolute power corrupts absolutely." This statement by Lord Acton, sent in a letter to Bishop Mandell Creighton on April 5, 1887, provides the basis for understanding the effects of power on the heads of state, and it furnishes insight into one of the main themes in the novel *Animal Farm*. Write a paper that shows how power affects the characters, the events and the outcome of the book.

Outline

I. Thesis Statement: Animal Farm *is a historical novel, set in England but dealing with the events leading up to and after the Russian Revolution of 1917. It illustrates the idea expressed by Lord Acton that power corrupts and absolute power corrupts absolutely. This abuse of power can be demonstrated by studying Napoleon's actions in the book.*

II. Power on Animal Farm before the Rebellion

    A. Man has absolute power, taking without producing

    B. Jones operates the Manor Farm with no regard for his animals

        1. Animals aren't fed

        2. Animals are slaughtered

        3. No animal lives its life to a natural end

        4. Animal families are broken up by the sale of the young

III. The Meeting

    A. Old Major holds the key to power: eliminate man

    B. The pigs are the leaders even before the Rebellion

        1. They are more clever than the others

        2. They are assertive, sitting in the front at the meeting

        3. They teach themselves to read

        4. They are the organizers forming various animal committees.

IV. The Rebellion

    A. Elimination of man creates a "power vacuum"

    B. Napoleon, Snowball and Squealer become the new leaders that fill the vacuum

    C. Pigs get special privileges—milk and apples

V. The Harvest

    A. Pigs are the supervisors

    B. They make the work schedules

    C. They move into the harness room

    D. Special privileges for the pigs are said to be necessary to keep Jones away

VI. The Windmill

    A. Napoleon and Snowball vie for control of the farm

    B. Napoleon eliminates the competition

        1. He uses the dogs to expel Snowball

        2. Squealer discredits Snowball

    C. Napoleon assumes the power to run Animal Farm

VII.   Changes on Animal Farm

    A.   Trade with the humans

        1.   The arrival of Mr. Whymper

        2.   The sale of a stack of hay

        3.   The sale of part of the wheat crop

        4.   Contract to sell eggs

    B.   Pigs move into farmhouse

    C.   Change in the Fourth Commandment concerning beds by the addition of the phrase "with sheets."

    D.   An end to voting at the Sunday meetings

    E.   The pigs become responsible for making all the work decisions

VIII. Force Equals Power

    A.   Mutiny of the Hens who object to the sale of their eggs

        1.   Starved out by Napoleon

        2.   Ended by unleashing the dogs

    B.   The "Great Purge"

        1.   Animal leaders opposed to Napoleon's policies are killed by the dogs

        2.   Boxer comes under attack for questioning Napoleon's condemnation of Snowball

IX.   More Changes

    A.   Changes in the Sixth Commandment allow Napoleon to kill other animals by adding the words "without cause."

    B.   Fifth Commandment allows the pigs to drink by the addition of the phrase "to excess" to the original Commandment

X.   Napoleon Sells Boxer to the Knacker

XI.   Return to "The Manor Farm"

    A.   Pigs are in complete control

    B.   They are the new aristocracy

      1.   They do no physical labor

      2.   Pigs carry whips

      3.   School is built for the baby pigs

  C. Animals can't tell the difference between man and pig

Topic #2

Animal Farm presents a classic blueprint for an individual's rise to power. It presents a step by step recipe for dictatorship and control. Write a paper that outlines the methods used by Napoleon and the pigs of their takeover of Animal Farm.

Outline

I.   Thesis Statement: Animal Farm *presents a recipe for dictatorship and control. The steps taken by Napoleon have been used by dictators from Julius Caesar to Adolf Hitler and Josef Stalin to achieve their ambitions.*

II.   Organization

  A. Develop a core of devout followers willing to die for the cause

  B. Develop a belief system—Animalism

  C. Identify a common enemy—man

III. Education

  A. The pigs teach themselves to read and write

  B. The other animals are kept ignorant

IV. Blind Obedience

  A. The sheep—"Four legs good, two legs bad."

  B. The dogs—They are devoted to Napoleon

  C. Boxer—"Napoleon is always right."

V.   Propaganda

  A. Slanted and false information—Squealer's ability to convince the animals—turn black into white

    B.   Rewriting history

    C.   Campaign against Snowball

    D.   Changing the rules

    E.   Changing the Seven Commandments

VI. Fear

    A.   The fear of Jones's return

    B.   Fear of the dogs

VII. Eliminate the Competition

    A.   Running Snowball off the farm

    B.   Eliminating the troublemakers

        1.   Killing the hen leaders of the mutiny

        2.   Killing the pigs who protest the end of the meetings

VIII. Scapegoating—Identify the cause of all the problems

    A.   Man—Frederick and Pilkington

    B.   Snowball—Jones's agent

IX. Force—Use of the dogs

Topic #3

    Animal Farm is a study of a dream betrayed. It begins with hope and it ends with despair. And although some things seem to change, the important things remain the same. Life for the animals only gets worse. Write a report that shows how and why this statement is true.

Outline

I.   Thesis Statement: Animal Farm *is the study of a dream betrayed. It begins with hope for the animals and ends with their miserable lives getting even worse.*

II.   Old Major's Dream

    A.   Man is the enemy

    B.   Eliminate man and life will be better

C. Work for the Rebellion

D. Avoid becoming like man when the Rebellion is achieved

III. The Rules for Utopia

A. Animalism

B. Equality

C. The unalterable Seven Commandments

IV. Cracks in the Dream

A. Preferential treatment for the pigs

B. Napoleon and Snowball struggle for power

C. Division of labor

1. The workers—Boxer and the others

2. The supervisors—the pigs

V. Abuses of Power

A. The expulsion of Snowball

B. Unleashing the dogs

C. Creating fear

D. Using force

VI. Changes in the Rules

A. Altering the unalterable Commandments

B. Rewriting history for Napoleon's personal glory

C. Destroying Snowball's contributions

VII. Selling out the Dream

A. Engaging in trade

B. Selling the eggs and murdering the chickens

C. Selling out Boxer for money to buy whiskey

VIII. The Pig-Men

A. Walking on two legs

B. Turning into men

Bibliography

Fitzpatrick, Sheila. *The Russian Revolution*. New York: Oxford University Press, 1982.

Gross, Miriam, Editor. *The World of George Orwell*. New York: Simon and Schuster, 1971.

Orwell, George. *Animal Farm*. A Signet Classic. New York: Penguin Books, 1971.

Rees, Richard. *George Orwell Fugitive from the Camp of Victory*. Chicago: Southern Illinois University Press, 1962.

Schapiro, Leonard. *The Russian Revolutions of 1917: The Origins of Modern Communism*. New York: Basic Books, Inc., 1984.